U.S. BATTLESHIP OPERATIONS
IN WORLD WAR I

U.S. BATTLESHIP OPERATIONS
IN WORLD WAR I

Jerry W. Jones

✳

Naval Institute Press
Annapolis, Maryland

Library of Congress Cataloging-in-Publication Data
Jones, Jerry W., 1964–
    U.S. battleship operations in World War I / Jerry W. Jones.
    p.   cm.
    Includes bibliographical references and index.
    ISBN 1-55750-411-3 (alk. paper)
    1. World War, 1914–1918—Naval operations, American.
    2. United States—History, Naval—20th century. I. Title.
    D589.U6J65   1998
    940.4'5973—dc21   97-46092

Printed in the United States of America on acid-free paper ∞

98 99 00 01 02 03 04 05   9 8 7 6 5 4 3 2
First printing
*Unless otherwise noted, all photos are courtesy
of the U.S. Naval Institute*

CONTENTS

*

Preface   vii

1   The Exorcism of Mahan's Ghost   *Anglo-American Naval Relations and the Role of the U.S. Battle Fleet in 1917*   1

2   Learning the Ropes   *U.S. Battleships with the Grand Fleet, December 1917 to June 1918*   22

3   Earning Respect   *U.S. Battleships with the Grand Fleet, July 1918 to the Surrender of the High Seas Fleet*   56

4   Lessons Learned   *U.S. Naval Gunnery and the Experience of World War I*   77

5   Defending the Transatlantic Convoys   *Planning for a Possible Battle Cruiser Raid, May to October 1918*   89

6   Sentinels   *Battleship Division Six at Berehaven, August to November 1918*   100

7   The Twilight of the Great White Fleet   *The Operations of U.S. Pre-Dreadnought Battleships during World War I*   108

Conclusion   127

Notes   131
Bibliography   157
Index   165

PREFACE

*

During World War I, the U.S. Navy assumed a subsidiary but significant role in the Allied naval effort. Germany and Great Britain were the major contenders of the naval war, fought mainly in the North Sea and the approaches to the channel ports. The contribution of the U.S. Navy was twofold: it ensured the continued supremacy of the Royal Navy and it helped protect the lines of communication to France, the decisive theater of the land war.

The submarine and its adversary, the destroyer, took on increased importance during the war. Nevertheless, the role of the opposing battle fleets remained vital. The supremacy of the Grand Fleet was the essential element of the blockade of Germany. Likewise, the High Seas Fleet was the power behind the U-boat blockade. Therefore, the rival fleets exerted an indirect, but crucial, influence on the outcome of the submarine campaign.

The crucible of the naval war was unrestricted submarine warfare. Most naval histories of the war naturally focus on the struggle against the U-boats and the only major fleet engagement of the war, the battle of Jutland. Other campaigns, however, are also important and are worthy of study. The treatment accorded the U.S. Navy during World War I is especially narrow, usually focusing on the operations of U.S. destroyers in European waters. The operations of other classes of warships are often ignored or treated as anecdotes.

U.S. battleships saw extensive service overseas during World War I. Twelve of America's sixteen dreadnought battleships and six of the pre-dreadnought battleships operated in the war zone. American battleships serving with the Grand Fleet participated in twenty-six sorties into the North Sea. The addition of U.S. battleships gave the Allies an unqualified superiority in battleships over the German fleet. This luxury allowed the Allies to divert to other duties their surplus battleships, which had been guarding against a sortie of the High Seas Fleet. Besides helping to maintain the naval blockade, U.S. battleships protected numerous troop and mercantile convoys in the North Sea and the Atlantic from German raiders.

The arrival of U.S. battleships in European waters not only strengthened the British Grand Fleet, it symbolized the U.S. commitment to the Allied effort. Although Navy Department and Admiralty heads did not always agree on strategy, tactical cooperation between the two navies, best represented by the amalgamation of a U.S. battleship division into the Grand Fleet, was an unprecedented success. Experience with the Grand Fleet, the most powerful fleet that had yet been assembled and one that had been made thoroughly efficient during three years of war, was invaluable in training U.S. officers and men and in developing future naval leaders. U.S. battleship operations in the war zone, then, led to increased efficiency of the U.S. battle fleet as a whole, while contributing to the Allied war effort and victory at sea.

The first chapter of this book traces diplomatic events leading to the U.S. Navy Department's decision to dispatch dreadnought battleships to European waters. The next two chapters discuss the introduction of Battleship Division Nine of the Atlantic Fleet into the British Grand Fleet. Chapter four examines the gunnery efficiency of U.S. battleships in comparison with British battleships and the impact of wartime experience on postwar gunnery. The two subsequent chapters deal with Anglo-American planning for a possible German battle cruiser raid against Atlantic convoys and the movement of Battleship Division Six to Berehaven, Ireland. The final chapter discusses the use of pre-dreadnought battleships as training ships, convoy escorts, and troop transports.

My research for this book is primarily based on records of the Department of the Navy in the National Archives and the Admiralty papers at the Public Record Office, London. Also important is the naval historical collection at the Naval War College, Newport, Rhode Island, and the private papers of principal naval leaders, located at the Library of Congress and the National Maritime Museum in Greenwich, England.

This book is a development of my doctoral dissertation, done at the University of North Texas. I am particularly indebted to three members of my doctoral committee, Dr. William Kamman, Dr. Bullitt Lowry, and Dr. Calvin Christman, who not only evaluated and improved my work but became my mentors. I am also grateful to Dr. Michael Simpson of the University of Wales, Swansea, for encouraging me in my project and for helping me navigate the Admiralty papers. I owe thanks also to Dr. Evelyn Cherpak at the Naval War College for her generous assistance, and to Mr. Paul Stillwell at the Naval Institute for providing me with several valuable oral histories. Finally, I want to thank my wife, Marie, for her advice, her support, and her encouragement every step of the way. It is my hope that this book is a suitable chronicle of a long neglected episode of U.S. naval history.

U.S. BATTLESHIP OPERATIONS
IN WORLD WAR I

1

THE EXORCISM OF MAHAN'S GHOST

Anglo-American Naval Relations and the Role
of the U.S. Battle Fleet in 1917

✳

When the United States entered World War I, the cause of the Entente hung in the balance. Unless Great Britain could counter the submarine menace, defeat seemed imminent. Shipping losses had depleted Britain's grain supplies and oil reserves. Deprived of food, the island nation would starve. Deprived of oil, the British war machine would grind to a halt. The crisis demanded immediate and concerted action, but British attempts to deal with the U-boats were ineffectual.

The United States was militarily unprepared when she joined the Entente coalition. President Woodrow Wilson's policy of armed neutrality had prevented any Anglo-American planning or cooperation beforehand. Divergent war aims and competing national interests then bedeviled Allied efforts toward cooperation. Only after several catastrophic defeats in 1917 would the close Anglo-American partnership be formed that would make victory possible in 1918.

Anglo-American cooperation was especially difficult in naval operations. Conflicting strategic ideas and a growing rivalry divided the two navies. Furthermore, American naval leaders feared that events would force Britain to accept an unfavorable peace with Germany, leaving the United States to continue the struggle alone against Germany, the world's second largest naval power. Even worse than this prospect was the possibility of a two-ocean conflict with both Germany and Japan. The signing of the Lansing-Ishii agreement would ease tensions with Japan, but U.S. naval leaders continued to fear a future conflict with Japan over the East Asian question and Japanese naval expansion, despite Japan's alignment against Germany.[1] The United States and Great Britain had to resolve these problems and concerns diplomatically before the U.S. Navy could play a larger role in the naval war.[2]

*

Immediately after President Wilson made the decision in late March to ask for a declaration of war, the Navy Department chose Rear Adm. William Sowden Sims to establish communication with the Admiralty because of his Canadian birth and close association with British officers.[3] Wilson instructed Sims to push the Admiralty to undertake a naval offensive or a close-blockade of the German submarine bases. Wilson scorned the British for "hunting hornets all over the farm and leaving the nest alone." The president also wanted the British to adopt the ancient practice of convoying to protect merchant shipping.

Before Sims left for London, Secretary of the Navy Josephus Daniels told Sims that he had been chosen in spite of his notorious Anglophilia.[4] (In 1911, then-Commander Sims had received a reprimand from President Taft for rashly promising U.S. support in the event of war with Germany to the Lord Mayor of London.[5]) The chief of naval operations, Adm. William Shepherd Benson, allegedly admonished Sims: "Don't let the British pull the wool over your eyes. It is none of our business pulling their chestnuts out of the fire. We would as soon fight the British as the Germans." Benson's stern advice, although probably motivated more by Sims's Anglophilia than by dislike of the British, exemplified the attitude of the Navy Department when the war began.[6]

While Sims was traveling to London, a joint Anglo-French mission arrived in Washington. Rear Adm. Maurice Ferdinand Albert de Grasset represented the Ministry of Marine, and Vice Adm. Sir Montague E. Browning represented the Admiralty.[7] The British made clear their opinion that the ability to protect shipping would decide the war. They also stressed their urgent desire for the United States to send large numbers of destroyers to Europe.[8] Both Daniels and Benson expressed their desire to cooperate in every way possible. They offered to immediately assume responsibility for the protection of shipping in the western Atlantic, the Gulf of Mexico, and much of the Caribbean. They also promised to maintain the China squadron and to form a South Atlantic squadron in the near future.[9]

The United States hesitated, however, about sending destroyers to Europe. German submarines were not much of a threat outside the war zone, but surface raiders were. The Navy Department decided to send only six destroyers for fear of weakening the screening forces of the U.S. battle fleet. The naval leadership considered any compromise of the integrity of the battle fleet to be a dangerous departure from U.S. naval policy.[10]

Admiral Benson and most of the Navy's leadership were firm disciples of Adm. Alfred Thayer Mahan. In 1890, Mahan had published a series of lectures on naval history that he had given at the United States Naval War College. Mahan's book, *The Influence of Sea Power upon History, 1660–1783*, became one of the most influential ever published in the United States.[11] His ideas about strategy and the nature of sea power laid the foundations of U.S. naval doctrine.

Mahan's purpose was to reawaken the country to the importance of sea power. The United States, preoccupied with westward expansion after the Civil War, had allowed the navy to atrophy. Mahan used the example of England's ascent to greatness to show that the United States could never be a world power without a great navy. Mahan's doctrine of sea power was both military and commercial; sea power and mercantilistic imperialism were synonymous. His policies expanded the role of the navy from coastal defense to a tool in power politics, an instrument and indication of national greatness.[12]

By reviewing the wars of trade in the seventeenth and eighteenth centuries, Mahan found support for the dictum that only a concentrated battle fleet could project sea power. Any division of the fleet invited disaster because detached units were easily defeated piecemeal. Mahan was equally emphatic about the primary mission of the battle fleet: to engage the enemy's fleet. He warned that any guerre de course, or commerce raiding stategy, amounted to abandoning any attempt to control the sea. Thus, Mahan not only provided justification for the construction of a battle fleet, he also laid down the strategic principles that governed how that fleet should be used.[13]

Naval planners continued to embrace Mahan's doctrine of fleet concentration long after his death. When the United States joined the Entente in 1917, the naval war plan was the same War Plan Black that had been developed prior to the Spanish-American War. Based upon Mahan's strategic ideas, War Plan Black presumed that the objective of war at sea would be to defend the Western Hemisphere from European aggression. The planners made no provision for the changes in technology, strategic situations, and mission that had occurred by the time of the U.S. entry into the First World War. The plan called for concentrating the battle fleet in the Gulf of Mexico to await a decisive battle with the enemy fleet, even though the British blockade now made such a scenario highly unlikely.[14] Fortunately, the naval leadership eventually compromised their Mahanite dogmatism in response to the military situation in 1917.

Washington did not have any idea how serious the shipping situation was for Britain until the Admiralty took Sims into their confidence. Upon arriving in London, Admiral Sims met with the First Sea Lord of the Royal Navy, Adm. Sir John Jellicoe.[15] (The two officers had first met in China in 1901. Both men had a common interest in naval gunnery, and they had become regular correspondents.) Admiral Jellicoe revealed to Sims that the Allied shipping losses to U-boats were nearly 600,000 tons per month. Astounded, Sims replied, "It looks as though the Germans are winning the war." Jellicoe calmly projected that the merchant marine would reach the level of endurance by November 1917 and England would then have to ask for terms. When Sims asked about the use of a convoy system to protect shipping from the U-boats, Admiral Jellicoe insisted that it was impossible because of the lack of escorts and the inability of merchant ships to keep station. Jellicoe could foresee no immediate solution to the problem.[16]

In response to these revelations, Sims fired off several cables to Washington. On 14 April, Sims explained the gravity of the situation and appealed for more merchant ships and destroyers, and on the eighteenth, cabled Daniels to repeat the plea for more destroyers. Sims did not believe that U.S. battleships were needed in the war zone, however, unless two divisions were based at Brest, France, to guard the channel against German raiders that slipped past the Grand Fleet.[17]

Sims was willing to transgress Mahan's "first commandment." He suggested that since it was impractical for the U.S. battle fleet to take part in the war, they did not need destroyer protection. Therefore, the Navy Department could release all destroyers for duty in the war zone. Sims further maintained that the president's plan for a close-blockade of German submarine bases was "wholly impractical." The Admiralty, he said, had studied the question and found that the danger to blockading forces from mines and torpedoes was too great.[18]

The next day, 19 April, Sims cabled Daniels to reinforce his earlier cables with a cry of, "More ships! More ships! More ships!" Sims also declared that he had managed to talk Prime Minister David Lloyd George out of the notion of a close-blockade (hardly calculated to please President Wilson!), and he forwarded the Admiralty's suggestion that the United States base dreadnoughts at Brest. From Brest, U.S. dreadnoughts would be well placed to support Allied naval forces in the English Channel, such as the Dover Patrol.[19]

During May 1917, a high-level mission composed of British Foreign Secretary Arthur Balfour and his naval advisor, Rear Adm. Dudley De Chair, visited Washington. Balfour hoped to convince the Americans to postpone their 1916 dreadnought building program in favor of building small craft for escort work. The United States would not countenance abandoning its capital ship program, however, because of the fear of a possible future two-ocean war with Germany and Japan. Nevertheless, the Navy Department did agreed to release twelve more destroyers for service overseas and promised another eighteen later.[20]

The American destroyers were a great help, but much more would have to be done. A change of tactics was needed to defeat the submarine. Sims began working to bring the British Admiralty around to adopting the convoy system. Sims found the prime minister sympathetic to the convoy idea. During a War Cabinet meeting in London on 25 April, Sims urged the adoption of the convoy system as the only way to defeat the U-boats. Lloyd George seconded Sims and criticized the Admiralty for their reluctance.[21] As a result of the continuing losses, and Lloyd George's personal intervention, the Admiralty finally began to implement a convoy system in early May 1917. They made it clear, however, that convoys would strain British resources and that more U.S. assistance would become necessary.[22]

Sims had an easier time bringing the Admiralty around to his views than he did the U.S. Navy Department. On 21 June 1917 Sims made another appeal to Daniels for more escorts. He had the temerity to add, "I consider it my duty to report that if we cannot offer more immediate actual assistance, even to the extent of sending the majority of the vessels patrolling our own coastlines which cannot materially affect the general situation, we will fail to render the service to the Allied cause which future history will show to have been necessary."[23] Daniels responded by assuring Sims of the department's willingness to cooperate and that every destroyer that could be spared from home waters, would be.[24]

Still not appeased, Sims gave Daniels a lecture on the merits of the convoy system. Warships would no longer have to scour the oceans in search of submarines, he said. The use of convoys would turn the tables and force the submarines to scatter in search of convoys, which would force them to run the risk of being sunk by escort ships. Sims stressed that the Admiralty would more enthusiastically embrace the convoy idea if sufficient antisubmarine craft were available. He again appealed for a change in strategy, urging that operations in home waters should no longer take precedence over operations in the war zone. Sims also suggested the need for cruiser and battleship escorts to protect against German surface raiders.[25] Daniels replied by religiously quoting the doctrine of Mahan: "The future position of the United States must in no way be jeopardized by any disintegration of our main fighting fleet." Daniels vigorously opposed any separation of a battle squadron or even any further weakening of the battle fleet's destroyer screen.[26] At this point, the United States had already sent twenty-eight of its fifty-one available destroyers to European waters.[27]

*

During July 1917 relations between the Navy Department and the Admiralty grew more strained. U.S. naval leaders and civilian observers grew more critical of the Royal Navy. The Admiralty seemed to lack a coherent strategy and refused to consider offensive operations. To Americans, the British policy of blockade evinced a total lack of élan. The British meanwhile viewed American ideas for a naval assault on submarine bases in the face of mines, torpedoes, and coastal artillery as nothing short of foolhardiness, bordering on insanity.[28]

President Wilson's frustration with the Admiralty began to harden after receiving a report by U.S. journalist and progressive Republican politician Winston Churchill (not the future British prime minister of that name). The president seemed to value Churchill's opinion on naval matters more than that of his own naval officers. Churchill, an 1894 Annapolis graduate who resigned his commission to pursue a writing career, earned Wilson's respect with a critical but constructive report on the Navy Department in the summer of 1917. Churchill had subsequently traveled to Britain to report on the Admiralty.[29] He harshly condemned the Lords of the Admiralty as unequal to the task. Churchill contended that the Admiralty "continued to ignore the main principle of naval strategy as laid down by Admiral Mahan and others, that it is the main business of a navy to fight, to be aggressive, to meet new problems as they arise." The solution, according to Churchill, was to "make American genius count."[30]

Wilson decided to prod the British into aggressive action. On 2 July, he wrote to Daniels, "As you and I agreed the other day, the British Admiralty had done nothing constructive in the use of their navy and I think it is time we were making and insisting upon plans of our own, even if we render some of the more conservative of our own naval advisors uncomfortable."[31] Beginning his campaign by writing directly to Sims in London, Wilson castigated the Admiralty for its lack of action. He expressed surprise that the Admiralty had failed to use Great Britain's naval superiority effectively: "In the presence of the present submarine emergency they are helpless to the point of panic." Wilson went on to state that boldness was in order, even at the cost of great losses. The president challenged Sims to tell him what, if anything, the Admiralty had accomplished. Implicit in this letter was Wilson's impression that Sims had become the mouthpiece of the Admiralty, rather than having an independent opinion.[32]

Although shaken by the president's strongly worded letter and thinly veiled rebuke, Sims defended the Admiralty's actions. He maintained that the British Grand Fleet was making the crucial antisubmarine campaign possible by keeping the High Seas Fleet bottled up in harbor. If not for the Grand Fleet, he said, the German fleet could drive all the Allied antisubmarine craft from the seas. Sims then went on to repeat his earlier views that a close-blockade was impracticable, that priority allocation of warships should be to the waters surrounding the United Kingdom, and that the United States should postpone construction of capital ships in favor of destroyers. To allay fears about future developments if the United States were to postpone its capital ship program, Sims declared, "We can always count on the Royal Navy."[33] Rather than further-ing the British cause, however, Sims's response merely strengthened the president's view that Sims was a pawn of the Admiralty.

The rumblings from Washington did not take long to reach London. On 5 July, Alfred Lord Northcliffe, head of a British mission to the United States, reported to the War Cabinet that the alleged inactivity of the Royal Navy in dealing with submarines was hampering diplomacy with the United States. He also explained that Benson maintained his support of the capital ship program because of his continued fear of a two-ocean war if Germany defeated the Allies and Japan took the oppor-tunity to attack U.S. interests in the Pacific. Lord Northcliffe suggested that the Admiralty might offer the United States the latest type of battle-ships and battle cruisers, ton for ton, in exchange for destroyers.[34]

Admiral Jellicoe defended the navy in his response to Lord North-cliffe: "The alleged inactivity of the navy in dealing with the submarine exists only in the imagination of those not acquainted with the facts." Concerning trading battleships for destroyers, Jellicoe insisted that Brit-ain needed all of her battleships as long as the German fleet remained intact.[35]

On 9 July, Daniels reaffirmed U.S. naval policy to Secretary of State Robert Lansing. Daniels stressed two points dogmatically. First, the United States would not jeopardize future security with any "disintegra-tion" of the main battle fleet. Second, the offensive must always be the dominant note in any general plan or strategy. Consequently, the United States was willing to send any destroyers or cruisers not needed at home, but was unwilling to separate any division from the main fleet. He would, however, send the entire U.S. fleet abroad if conditions war-ranted.[36]

After receiving a copy of Daniels's statement of policy, Sims wrote a lengthy letter explaining his views to him. In his letter, Sims displayed uncharacteristic tact. The letter also reveals the conflicting perspectives that often hamper cooperation between a theater commander and the leadership at home. Sims stated that he was operating under the as-sumption that the mission was to promote cooperation with the Allies to defeat the common enemy. He could not comprehend why questions of postwar U.S. security should take precedence over the immediate war effort. Unlike more nationalistic officers such as Benson, Sims did not burden himself with questions of long-range policy and national self-interest; rather, he viewed America's fortunes as inextricably linked with those of the Allies. He believed that a victorious Entente coalition would automatically guarantee future security.[37]

Sims argued that the U.S. fleet was an auxiliary, or reserve, of the British Grand Fleet. Sims acknowledged that such a view could be seen as a "disintegration of the fleet" and that caution was only natural. Nevertheless, he argued that the U.S. Navy could give maximum support to the Allies without the dreaded disintegration of the fleet. Sims explained that the nature of the Allied lines of communication, coupled with the enemy's lack of available submarines, restricted the enemy's main effort to European waters. Occasional U-boat attacks outside the war zone were only meant to scatter the limited antisubmarine craft. Therefore, the war would be won or lost in European waters.[38]

Sims pointed out that it would not be practical to send the entire U.S. battle fleet to the war zone because there were not enough small craft to both provide the fleet with an adequate screen and serve as escorts for merchant ship convoys. Further, the British could not supply the U.S. fleet with oil because of the acute shortage in England. Sims maintained that since the United States could not use its battle fleet in the war zone, the Navy Department should release all screening vessels for antisubmarine work. Considering that the stronger Grand Fleet kept the High Seas Fleet contained, moving all of the U.S. destroyers into the war zone would not constitute a disintegration of the main fleet; the destroyers would remain between the enemy and the battle fleet. Sims extended his argument to include sending battleship units to serve with the Grand Fleet. He maintained that they would merely form advance units, which would always remain in a position to fall back to the main battle fleet.[39] Clearly, Sims's interpretation flew in the face of Mahanite dogma and the Navy Department remained unconvinced.

After visiting the Grand Fleet with Sims on 19 July 1917, Jellicoe requested that the United States send a division of four coal-burning dreadnoughts, along with a screen of six destroyers, to serve with the Grand Fleet.[40] This would allow the Admiralty to detach five *King Edward VII*–class pre-dreadnoughts from the Grand Fleet. The *King Edward VIIs* would in turn replace older pre-dreadnought battleships, which would be paid off. The Admiralty could then use the crews of the decommissioned ships to man new antisubmarine craft. (Like the U.S. Navy, the Royal Navy suffered from a chronic shortage of experienced officers and seamen.) Thus, not only would the replacement of obsolete pre-dreadnoughts with newer U.S. battleships materially strengthen the Grand Fleet, the scheme would also aid the struggle against the U-boat.[41]

The Navy Department rejected the request despite Sims's endorsement. With the support of the commander in chief of the Atlantic Fleet, Adm. Henry T. Mayo, Benson decided that the U.S. fleet should remain fully manned and ready for battle as a unit. In keeping with the doctrine of Mahan, the fleet would remain concentrated. Furthermore, Benson told Sims that the Navy Department would send no U.S. battleships until the British developed an aggressive plan of action. In effect, the battleships were diplomatic bargaining chips, to be used to spur the Royal Navy into offensive action.[42]

*

By the end of July, the Admiralty and the Navy Department were at an impasse over the offensive-action issue. To improve relations with the Entente navies, the Navy Department sent Admiral Mayo to Europe. A secondary purpose for the mission was to check on Admiral Sims, who President Wilson believed no longer represented U.S. interests. Wilson hoped that the Mayo mission would spur the Allies to action and make the United States the senior partner in an aggressive naval campaign. Daniels favored the mission because he was "getting tired of playing second fiddle to the British by meeting all their demands."[43]

The Mayo mission and a subsequent naval conference at last put the Allies on the path toward compromise and cooperation. Mayo began preliminary discussions with the Admiralty on 29 August 1917. He frankly told the First Lord of the Admiralty, Sir Eric Geddes, that the United States wanted a larger role in the naval war. He made it clear that Wilson wanted a more aggressive policy, quoting the president's admonition: "You can't make omelettes without breaking eggs, war is made up of taking risks." Mayo also told the First Lord that Wilson had expressed a desire to "get more cooperation from [the Admiralty] both now and in the future."[44]

Stung by President Wilson's implied charge that they lacked both the will to undertake determined action and the spirit of cooperation, the

Admiralty vigorously defended their naval policy to Mayo. The British illustrated the futility of a naval offensive against German U-boat bases by showing Mayo confidential charts that marked the locations of shore batteries and minefields surrounding the German coast. The Admiralty also presented figures to show that the margin of superiority of the British fleet over the German fleet was much less than commonly presumed. In terms of destroyers, in fact, the German fleet was clearly superior.[45] Jellicoe again broached the idea of sending U.S. battleships to serve with the Grand Fleet.[46] Mayo forwarded the request to Daniels, at the same time reporting that Sims was doing a good job in London.[47]

The initiative for the Mayo mission developed into the Inter-Allied Naval Conference of 4–5 September, at which Mayo was the U.S. representative.[48] During the conference, the British responded to U.S. criticism with a plan for a close offensive in German waters. The Admiralty proposed to sink old warships to block German channels. The British asked that the United States contribute twelve of her oldest battleships and eight of her oldest cruisers.[49] Admiral Mayo submitted the request to Benson, but added his belief that nothing would ever come of it and that it had little chance of success.[50] Faced with the cost of the long-awaited offensive plan, the Navy Department lost enthusiasm for a close-blockade and concurred with Mayo about its impracticability. The Admiralty, for its part, happily let the matter drop.[51]

As an alternative to the close-blockade, the British suggested laying a mine barrage in the North Sea between Norway and Scotland to deny German submarines access to the Atlantic. It was understood that this would be primarily an American effort. This plan satisfied Wilson that the "hornets would be shut up in their nests," and the Admiralty's willingness to meet the Americans halfway on the idea of an offensive removed a major stumbling block to Anglo-American naval cooperation.[52]

After the naval conference, the Admiralty gave Mayo a white paper describing and defending their naval policy. According to this paper, their first priority was to use a naval blockade to bring pressure on the enemy. The second was to protect the sea communications of the Allies and Allied trade. The Grand Fleet was the basis of Allied naval power and the hinge of this strategy. By denying the German fleet access to the sea, the Grand Fleet provided security to all the smaller warships engaged in protecting trade and hunting submarines. The British also pointed out that although the Grand Fleet "adopts a waiting attitude," its destroyer screen was used in antisubmarine work as much as possible.[53]

Mayo did not consider the white paper evidence of a comprehensive policy, but rather a summary of past activities. The defensive nature of the Admiralty policy struck Mayo as overly passive. He also recognized that the role of trade protection (defense) consumed most of the Royal Navy's assets other than the Grand Fleet. Nevertheless, Mayo was pleased to report that the Admiralty had indicated a growing appreciation of the necessity for more energetic offensive measures.[54]

Before leaving London, Admiral Mayo asked the Admiralty for a statement of contemplated changes to their naval policy and of future assistance desired from the United States. The British replied that they intended to increase offensive operations against submarines—which would require minelayers and numerous mines from the United States.[55] In addition, they needed more destroyers and merchant ships. Further, the Admiralty still hoped for the addition of U.S. dreadnoughts to the Grand Fleet. The scope of the antisubmarine campaign meant paying off more capital ships to provide officers and crews for the 119 destroyers then under construction in Britain. The Admiralty offered that, should the U.S. government decide to send the battleships, the ships could work together as a division or a battle squadron.[56]

In the wake of the Mayo mission, relations between the Navy Department and its theater commander, Admiral Sims, improved significantly.[57] Sims was encouraged because he was certain that his views would be vindicated. To his confidant in the Navy Department, Assistant Chief of Naval Operations Capt. William Veazie Pratt, Sims wrote: "I am sure that when Admiral Mayo returns and you people have had time to go over his reports . . . you will have a much clearer idea of the situation over here than you have had up to the present time."[58]

Sims took the opportunity to improve his relations with Benson. Pratt had warned Sims that his constant criticism had irritated the chief of naval operations. Sims attempted to make amends by expressing his appreciation for the difficulty of Benson's position. He explained that his criticism was the result of impatience, not ill feeling. Sims was so concerned about his standing in the Navy Department that he pointed out the damage to relations with the Admiralty that would result if the department should replace him.[59]

Benson responded to Sims's overture with a candid and heartfelt letter. He admitted that he had asked Pratt to stop showing him Sims's letters because, "I was afraid that the constant spirit of criticism and complaint that pervaded them . . . would gradually produce a state of mind that was undesirable, to say the least." Benson admitted his surprise that Sims would direct his complaints to a subordinate rather than to Benson himself, and indicated that this habit of going behind his back accounted for the poor relations between the two. Benson also mentioned his disappointment that neither Sims nor the Admiralty had put forward a plan of operations. He felt the Admiralty was treating the Navy Department as nothing more than a source of matériel. The chief of naval operations went on to state that the reason for the department's unwillingness to send a portion of the battleship force to serve with the Grand Fleet was the lack of an operational plan. Benson ended his letter by appealing for better cooperation and understanding.[60]

Benson's letter resulted in detente between the chief of naval operations and the theater commander. Sims refrained from expressing too many criticisms of the Navy Department for the duration of the war. After the war, however, the veneer of good relations between Sims and Benson would end. In 1920 Sims brought allegations of wartime incompetence against the Navy Department before the Senate Committee on Naval Affairs. The hearings made national headlines and divided the Navy into factions. Sims's charges lacked substance, and the Senate report absolved the Navy Department. It was fortunate for the U.S. war effort that the dissension between Sims and the Navy Department did not break out into open hostilities until after the armistice.[61]

The Mayo mission significantly improved the relationship between the Navy Department and the Admiralty. Personal communications were established and there was a general clearing of the air. First Lord Geddes contacted Secretary Daniels to express appreciation for Admiral Mayo's visit and the greater understanding and communication the visit had fostered. Geddes encouraged the secretary to express his views directly to the Admiralty in an effort to bring about better cooperation, acknowledging that there was no substitute for closer communication between the Navy Department and the Admiralty. Further, he requested that, as a follow-up to the Mayo mission, Admiral Benson travel to London for talks with his opposite number, Admiral Jellicoe.[62]

Jellicoe also took the opportunity of Mayo's visit to establish direct correspondence with Benson. In a conciliatory letter, he expressed appreciation for U.S. support and discussed the accomplishments of the Mayo mission. He addressed Benson's concern over the British lack of action by pointing out that the Royal Navy took offensive action against any enemy vessels it could find. He defended British policy, arguing that "it takes two to make a fight, and our difficulty throughout the war has been that, except in one or two exceedingly rare occasions, the second party to the fight has not been there."[63] In his reply to Jellicoe, Benson was magnanimous: "For many years, I have hoped for the day when our countries would be more closely united in the common cause for the good of mankind."[64]

Sims wrote to Benson to express his continuing anxiety over the Navy Department's hesitation in granting the Admiralty's request for battleships to serve with the Grand Fleet. He admitted that he did not really understand what "disintegration of the fleet" meant and did not see a way for the battle fleet to participate in the war as a unit, but repeated his argument that a U.S. battleship division serving in European waters would merely be an advance force between the U.S. battle fleet and the enemy. However, someone, presumably Benson, wrote in the margin, "But this is a division of the main force which is always faulty if not fatal." Mahan's dogma was still the pure faith in the Navy Department.[65]

In a letter to Pratt, Sims pointed out that German battle cruisers under construction were nearing completion. In Sims's opinion, this was another good reason to reinforce the Grand Fleet with U.S. battleships. Sims was so convinced of the urgency of granting the Admiralty's request to send the ships that he said, "I cannot bring myself to believe that any other decision could be made by our government."[66]

In October 1917 the General Board of the Navy held hearings on the British request that a squadron of dreadnoughts join the Grand Fleet. The testimony of some of the board's witnesses revealed that concern over Japanese intentions was a major reason to retain the battleships on the East Coast. On the other hand, Captain Pratt, testifying before the board, urged that the Navy Department honor the British request. Reassured by the results of the Lansing-Ishii agreement, Pratt hoped that the Japanese would follow the U.S. example and send their own reinforcements to Europe. Another General Board witness and Navy Department staff officer, Capt. Frank H. Schofield, also supported the dispatch of U.S. battleships to Europe. He suggested that to grant the British request would indicate American good will and also place Great Britain in America's debt. Consequently, he argued, the United States could persuade the British not to transfer any warships to the Japanese that could eventually endanger American interests in the Pacific. Admiral Benson, however, did not yet agree with the position of Pratt and Schofield.[67]

In late October, Wilson received a letter from the American journalist Churchill. Churchill had visited London during the naval conference as an independent observer and sent his assessment of the results. Among other points, Churchill suggested that the United States should comply with the British request for four coal-burning dreadnoughts. He accepted the Admiralty's concern about the slim numerical superiority of British dreadnoughts to German dreadnoughts, especially in light of Germany's vast superiority in the number of destroyers.

Churchill also suggested using older U.S. battleships to protect convoys against German surface raiders.[68] This was a radical departure from Mahan's doctrine of fleet concentration, but the war at sea was evolving in ways that Mahan had not foreseen. With naval orthodoxy seemingly unequal to the task, radical new ideas were gaining credence. Suggesting the use of battleships to escort convoys would have been considered blasphemous earlier in the war, but was not so strange in the conditions of late 1917. Although no action was taken on the journalist's suggestion at the time, U.S. pre-dreadnought battleships would be escorting American troop convoys a year later.

*

Earlier, in September 1917 while Admiral Mayo was still in London, the British suggested holding a general conference to promote cooperation among the Allies. The success of the German U-boats and the failure of French and British offensives on the Western Front pointed to the need for greater coordination.[69] At first, President Wilson was unenthusiastic about U.S. representation at the conference because of his fear of diplomatic entanglements that could compromise his plan for an enlightened peace settlement. It became increasingly apparent, however, that there would be no enlightened peace if the war was not won. Wilson acquiesced after his closest advisor, Col. Edward M. House, assured him that only military measures, and not war aims, would be discussed at the conference. The president asked Colonel House to head the delegation, with Admiral Benson as the naval representative.[70]

On 7 November 1917 the House mission arrived in Britain. It could not have come at a more critical time. The Austrians had just defeated the Italian army at Caporetto and the Bolsheviks had seized power in Russia. The situation looked very dark for the Allies, and the gravity of the situation gave added impetus for closer cooperation. Benson immediately began discussions with the Admiralty, communicating the intentions of the United States to make a greater naval contribution, but only according to well-defined plans. Benson was considerate, but frankly reported his dissatisfaction with the defensive policies of the Admiralty. Nevertheless, Benson was willing to consider Admiralty views with an open mind.[71]

After a few days in London, having become more familiar with conditions in the war zone, Benson moved closer to the views of the British Admiralty and Sims. On 10 November, after three days of discussions, the chief of naval operations cabled Daniels to recommend that the Navy Department promptly dispatch four coal-burning dreadnoughts for service with the Grand Fleet.[72]

Benson wrote a lengthy memorandum explaining his decision to reverse the earlier policy. First of all, he had become convinced that the British really needed reinforcements to provide the Grand Fleet with a safe margin of superiority. Benson noted, "If, in any encounter, it should be indicated that the outcome would have been more favorable or more decisive had more Allied forces been available, it would be difficult to explain the absence of our ships."[73]

Benson was always primarily interested in the long-range interests of his country. Regarding the possible impact on domestic policy if U.S. battleships did not participate in the war, Benson observed: "Whatever may be the present situation, the future of the United States will depend in large measure upon the strength, the training, and the prestige of the Navy. A decision now averse to sending any of our battleships to the front will be invoked in the future against the building of large vessels." Benson was also concerned about the foreign policy implications if the ships were not sent: "The major consideration is prestige. . . . There should be no possibility of an impression, at home or abroad, among the hostile, Allied or neutral, that we are performing an auxiliary or secondary part in the military prosecution of the war."

Benson ended his memorandum by modifying his earlier interpretation of Mahan's commandment of fleet concentration: "The principle not to divide the fleet does not apply to this matter in my opinion. It would apply to the portion of the fleet necessarily kept in American waters by logistical considerations, rather than to a division to join the Grand Fleet."[74]

This change of heart by his trusted naval advisor finally convinced Secretary Daniels to send the dreadnoughts. The Navy Department chose to dispatch Battleship Division Nine of the Atlantic Fleet, composed of the *New York, Florida, Delaware,* and *Wyoming.* These ships, the best coal-burners in the fleet, were under the flag of Adm. Hugh Rodman.[75] After five months of debate, the Navy Department finally granted the British request and U.S. dreadnoughts began their journey across the North Atlantic.

With Mahanite dogma compromised, the Admiralty hoped to persuade the Navy Department to send the remaining ten American coal-burning dreadnoughts to serve with the Grand Fleet as well. Except for the two squadrons on the flanks of the battle line, which had four ships each, a British battle squadron comprised eight ships. Ten U.S. dreadnoughts would form a complete squadron, allowing for the continual refit and docking of two of the American ships. The addition of another battle squadron to the Grand Fleet would allow the British to station a battle squadron further south to guard against any German battle cruiser raids on the eastern coast of England. At present, this mission was being performed by the British battle cruiser fleet, based at Rosyth, 200 miles south of the main fleet anchorage at Scapa Flow. The danger in this disposition was that the Germans could decide to use their fast battleships in conjunction with their battle cruisers to raid the East Coast. The British battle cruiser fleet would not be strong enough to deal with such a powerful raiding force.[76]

Another reason behind the Admiralty request for additional American dreadnoughts was the desire to take advantage of a Norwegian base, should Norway enter the war. The Admiralty planners realized that if the British battle fleet were based at Stavanger, Norway, it would be closer to the Skagerrak and Heligoland than if it were based at either Rosyth or Scapa Flow, making it easier to intercept any sortie of the High Seas Fleet. The Grand Fleet would also be better placed to support the North Sea mine barrage, making it a much more effective obstacle to German submarines. This plan also required additional battleships to maintain a battle squadron on the English east coast. A strong force there, probably on the Humber, would prevent the Germans from drawing the Grand Fleet south by the threat of a diversionary raid. According to the Admiralty, the addition of more U.S. battleships would make the difference between sufficient and insufficient forces to make the plan work.[77]

To gain American acceptance of the plan, the Admiralty attempted to answer any possible objections that could arise to the use of additional U.S. battleships in the North Sea. Supplying oil to the latest U.S. oil-burning battleships would be a problem, they acknowledged, but there was no shortage of coal in the British Isles for coal-burning vessels. The Admiralty also recognized that the U.S. fear of attack from Japan could necessitate retention of the battle fleet in American waters. They therefore proposed to persuade the Japanese government to send its battle cruisers to Europe, using the promise of replacing any losses from enemy action as inducement.[78] The dispatch of Japanese ships to European waters would lessen the naval threat to the United States and remove that objection to moving more U.S. battleships to Europe.

To the Navy Department, neither the remote possibility of acquiring a Norwegian base nor the British desire to guard against German raids on England's east coast justified the dispatch of additional battleships to Europe. The threat of German battle cruisers escaping into the Atlantic to ravage U.S. troop convoys did, however. The Navy Department decided to dispatch three ships of Battleship Division Six of the Atlantic Fleet to Berehaven, Ireland. Further British requests were denied. Beyond Division Nine serving with the Grand Fleet and Division Six based in Ireland, no other U.S. battleships would be permanently stationed in European waters during the war.[79]

Along with the decision to send some U.S. battleships to Europe, the Navy Department made other decisions that improved cooperation with the Admiralty. Daniels approved Benson's recommendation for an

Allied Naval Council and a joint naval planning section in Sims's office. The Allied Naval Council was intended as an organ to coordinate naval policy and advise the Supreme War Council. Although formed to help prosecute the war, the main contribution of the Allied Naval Council would be in drawing up the terms of the naval armistice, which provided for the internment of the defeated High Seas Fleet at Scapa Flow. More successful in developing wartime naval policy was the Joint Naval Planning Section in London. Joint planning helped to ensure that Allied naval policy better reflected the interests of the United States and made the U.S. Navy a more equal partner in the naval war.[80]

The Navy Department also softened its demand for an offensive strategy, removing much of the dissension between the Americans and the British. In a statement of naval policy, the chief of naval operations made a major concession to the British by recognizing the usefulness of the Admiralty's blockade policy. He agreed that a more effective blockade, including a North Sea mine barrage, would force the enemy either to confine its submarines or to support the submarines with the surface fleet. The latter action would, the naval leaders hoped, result in the long-awaited decisive fleet action.[81]

The British in turn offered several major concessions. They agreed to make another attempt to close the straits of Dover and they agreed to undertake a joint naval offensive with the Americans.[82] The Benson mission finally accomplished what had been lacking in Anglo-American naval relations—communication and compromise.

✳

In retrospect, it is easy to criticize Chief of Naval Operations Benson for his stubborn refusal to grant the British request for battleship reinforcements. It must be remembered, however, that most of the naval leadership of that time was imbued with the same rigid Mahanism. Moreover, Benson owed his position to his support for civilian control of the Navy. In 1915 there had been a movement to create a naval general staff, which would have effectively removed civilian control from naval operations. After the Wilson administration refused to create such a staff, Republicans introduced legislation to create an Office of Naval Operations in the Navy Department. Secretary of the Navy Daniels managed to have the law amended to limit the jurisdiction of the chief of naval operations to fleet operations only. The General Board of the Navy and the various bureau chiefs remained subject only to the secretary of the navy. Daniels then passed over all of the admirals and appointed a loyal captain, William Benson, as the first chief of naval operations. Thus Benson did not have very much latitude, and Daniels made the final decisions.[83]

It is to Benson's credit that he was able to reverse his earlier views after becoming convinced that it was in the national interest to do so. It required courage to detach a unit from the battle fleet, because Mahan's concept of fleet concentration was widely regarded as sacred and immutable. Benson's more liberal interpretation of fleet concentration broke precedent and had the long-term effect of making U.S. naval policy more flexible. Although many of Mahan's ideas are timeless and govern naval strategy to this day, the Navy Department never again interpreted Mahan's ideas as rigidly as in 1917.[84] Furthermore, Benson's fear of Japanese intentions was legitimate and his concerns about postwar U.S. security were sound and prescient.

Admiral Sims must share some of the blame for the haggling and delay. He refused to be sensitive to concerns of national security and national interest. As a result, Sims had better relations with the British than with his own country's Navy Department. Doubts about his independence of mind caused the Navy Department to view him as an alarmist, and Sims managed to alienate himself from his superiors through his constant criticism. Had he been more forthright with his chief, rather than dealing through Benson's assistant, Captain Pratt, Sims might have won the Navy Department over to his views much earlier.

The main reason the questions of Anglo-American naval strategy took so long to iron out goes beyond the actions of any particular individual. The United States and Great Britain were former adversaries and had never before cooperated as allies. Moreover, the two navies had different traditions and strategic priorities that often conflicted. The two nations had to compromise their individual national interests to some extent for the benefit of the naval war effort.

The debate over whether to send a division of U.S. battleships to Europe illustrates the conflict over naval strategy between the two allies. Battleships, and how they should be used, were at the heart of the controversy. Before U.S. battleships could play an active role in the naval war, both the U.S. and the Royal navies had to modify their naval policies in the interest of cooperation.

Coalition warfare cannot be effectively waged without consensus over strategy. The arrival of the U.S. dreadnoughts in Britain is significant because it signaled that consensus had been reached among the naval and civilian leaders of the United States and Great Britain.

2

LEARNING THE ROPES

U.S. Battleships with the Grand Fleet,
December 1917 to June 1918

✳

Some historians have portrayed the dreadnoughts of the British Grand Fleet as idly swinging at their anchors while the submarine war raged around them.[1] This view implies that the battle fleet was superfluous. Actually, the Grand Fleet was the real power behind the antisubmarine campaign. Had the German High Seas Fleet eliminated the primacy of the Grand Fleet at Jutland in 1916, the Germans would have been free to drive all of the antisubmarine craft from the seas. Consequently, the Allies would have lost the submarine campaign and eventually the war. Furthermore, the naval blockade was a major factor in Germany's defeat, and the Grand Fleet was the ultimate power behind the smaller warships that enforced the blockade. And the ships of the Grand Fleet were far from idle. Constant readiness was required to keep the High Seas Fleet in confinement.

In evaluating the role of the American squadron with the Grand Fleet, Sir Frederick Maurice states, "There is little to be gained from studying the problems of tactical cooperation of Allied fleets in battle, because they were never tested in battle."[2] He completely ignored the crucial role that the naval blockade played in bringing about the final defeat of Germany, however. Because a decisive fleet engagement was not necessary for victory, it was sufficient for the Grand Fleet to remain passively superior.

Although the American battleships with the Grand Fleet never met the German High Seas Fleet in battle, they were active in North Sea military operations. The American squadron not only helped enforce the blockade, it also escorted important Scandinavian convoys through some of the most hazardous waters in the war zone and provided protection for the minelaying forces in the North Sea.

The superiority of the Grand Fleet allowed the protection of North Sea commerce and offensive mining operations while also maintaining the blockade of the German fleet. The addition of the U.S. battleships removed any doubt about the superiority of the Grand Fleet.

*

When the U.S. battleships arrived in European waters, a cloud still hung over the British Grand Fleet as a result of the battle of Jutland. The only major fleet action of the war, Jutland had been disappointingly inconclusive and had revealed serious matériel deficiencies in the British fleet. It had shown the structural weakness of British battle cruisers and the inferiority of British shells.

The war against commerce imposed considerable demands upon Grand Fleet resources. A. J. Marder lists three duties that necessitated the detachment of numerous light forces from the Grand Fleet: the use of Grand Fleet destroyers for convoy escort and antisubmarine patrol; the need for destroyers and light cruisers to protect minelaying operations in Heligoland Bight; and the use of heavy ships to protect Scandinavian convoys from German surface raiders.[3] If the Germans chose the most advantageous moment to sortie, many of the Grand Fleet's dispersed units would not have time to rejoin the main fleet before battle.[4]

These considerations prompted Adm. Sir David Beatty, commander in chief of the Grand Fleet, to draft a memorandum to the Admiralty outlining the limitations imposed on the fleet and his proposed future Grand Fleet policy. Beatty pointed out that the paper strength of the Grand Fleet was considerably greater than its real strength. For example, even though the British possessed nine battle cruisers opposed to the enemy's six, Beatty considered only *Lion, Princess Royal,* and *Tiger* fit to be in the line against the German battle cruisers. Furthermore, some of the deficiencies revealed at Jutland remained. Armor-piercing shells capable of penetrating German armor would not be available for the fleet's main armament until the summer of 1918. If the Grand Fleet were forced to accept battle on the enemy's terms, there was the real possibility of another indecisive engagement, or even a defeat.[5]

Beatty also detailed the draining effect of convoy duty on Grand Fleet strength. Unlike British destroyers and light cruisers, the German light forces had no duties to perform other than fleet operations. The Germans, then, could keep their light forces concentrated and in a high state of readiness. The Grand Fleet would go into battle with a screening force that was inferior. Beatty considered the Grand Fleet superior in battleships, though he knew that some attrition before battle would be inevitable. Given the advantage of choosing the time and place to offer battle, the enemy could position numerous submarines and mines on the lines of approach of the British fleet. In addition, battleships covering the Scandinavian convoys would most likely be unable to join the main fleet in time for battle; Beatty considered them permanent deductions from the battle line.[6]

Admiral Beatty identified two missions for the Grand Fleet: to defeat the enemy fleet and to control communications in the North Sea. With the resources then available to the Grand Fleet, he argued, these two missions were incompatible. The Grand Fleet could only accomplish one at the expense of the other. He concluded, "Accepting the principle that trade must be protected, the deduction to be drawn is that the correct strategy of the Grand Fleet is no longer to endeavor to bring the enemy to action at any cost, but rather to contain him in his bases until the general situation becomes more favorable to us. This does not mean that action should be avoided if conditions favor us, or that our role should be passive and purely defensive."[7]

Sir Rosslyn Wester Wemyss, who had replaced Admiral Jellicoe as the First Sea Lord in December 1917, and Sir Eric Geddes, the First Lord of the Admiralty, endorsed Beatty's policy. Wemyss said that Beatty's paper "entirely confirms the opinion that I have formed since my advent to the Admiralty."[8] The board of the Admiralty drew up a statement of future naval policy that closely followed Beatty's proposals, and the First Lord submitted it to the War Cabinet. On 18 January 1918, the War Cabinet formally approved the Admiralty policy.[9] This new strategy was not really new, but in effect was the same prudent strategy Beatty had followed during 1917. What was new about Grand Fleet policy was that Beatty had spelled out the reasons for his strategy, and he had obtained formal approval from the Admiralty and the War Cabinet.[10]

Considering the demands on Grand Fleet resources, the addition of a division of U.S. battleships was important and needed. The arrival of the U.S. division reduced the deficiencies in the Grand Fleet in several ways. Having a shortage of trained personnel, the Royal Navy, with the arrival of the U.S. ships, was able to pay off older battleships to release those crews for duty on destroyers. In addition, the arrival of the U.S. battleships gave the British enough capital ship strength to protect the Scandinavian convoys with a heavy covering force. The Admiralty probably would not have done so without the added measure of battleship superiority.

✳

Rear Adm. Hugh Rodman, known in the Navy Department as "Uncle Hugie," assumed command of the Atlantic Fleet's Battleship Division Nine on 13 November 1917. Rodman was a Kentuckian known for his storytelling and his seamanship. Secretary Daniels probably chose Rodman to command the American squadron with the Grand Fleet because of his reputation for expert seamanship, but his engaging wit and talent for spinning a good yarn proved equally important in achieving the smooth integration of his squadron into the British Grand Fleet. John McCrea, then a young lieutenant in command of the *New York*'s number three turret and later commander of the *Iowa* during World War II, remembered Rodman as "an excellent shiphandler, quick-witted, excellent at cribbage, played a good game of bridge. . . . He considered himself an authority on the qualities of Kentucky bourbon whiskey, and yielded to no one when it came to making a mint julep." What impressed McCrea most, however, was Rodman's skill in leading and grooming subordinates: "He liked young officers, watched their development with great interest, gave them responsibility, often in excess of their experience, and watched their responses to this increased responsibility." Under his guidance, many of Rodman's officers gained some of the most valuable experience of their careers while attached to the Grand Fleet. Rodman proved an excellent choice for such an important and sensitive post.[11]

The commanders of Rodman's battleships were also respected senior officers. Capt. Charles F. Hughes, who became chief of naval operations in 1927, commanded Rodman's flagship, the *New York*. Hughes was "a fine sailorman," who rarely went ashore and could not understand why others should.[12] Capt. Archibald H. Scales commanded the *Delaware*,

Capt. Thomas Washington, the *Florida*, and Capt. Henry A. Wiley, a future commander in chief of the Atlantic Fleet, the *Wyoming*.[13]

Once Secretary Daniels had made the decision to send Division Nine to European waters, he took very little interest in its operations. Daniels delegated all responsibility for determining the details and conditions of the division's deployment to Benson, the chief of naval operations.[14] Benson's deployment orders to Rodman were brief. After joining the British fleet, Division Nine would be under the operational control of the commander in chief of the Grand Fleet. In all other matters, the division would remain subject to the Navy Department and U.S. Navy organization and chain of command. Rodman's superior was Adm. William S. Sims, commander in chief of U.S. Navy Forces in European Waters.[15] The Navy Department issued all further instructions to Rodman through Sims's office in London.[16]

Battleship Division Nine left Lynn Haven Roads at 1500 on 25 November. With the *New York* in the lead, followed by the *Wyoming, Florida*, and *Delaware*, and with the new U.S. destroyer *Manley* as escort, Division Nine stood out of the Virginia Capes and set a course for Scapa Flow in the Orkney Islands. The ships sailed in line ahead at night, line abreast during the day. The weather was bad from the beginning of the voyage, and it grew worse. On 26 November, a northwester hit the ships. The storm brought sleet, hail, and snow, but soon blew itself out.

Three days later, on Thanksgiving Day, the division ran into a severe gale off the Grand Banks. Captain Wiley recalled, "At the height of the gale, it blew as hard as I have ever seen it, and the seas were the worst I could recollect."[17] Lieutenant McCrea, aboard the *New York*, remembered the storm as the worst he experienced in twenty-two years of sea duty. Storm damage allowed over 250 tons of seawater to flood the *New York*'s chain lockers and forward compartments. Soon the bow of the ship was hardly rising with the sea. Bailing lines worked around the clock for three days to keep the *New York* from foundering.[18]

During the gale on the night of 30 November, the *Delaware, Florida*, and *Manley* could no longer keep station, and lost contact with the division. The topmasts of all four battleships were carried away in the storm, putting their radios out of commission. Station keeping was difficult and dangerous. Searchlights and navigation lights worked only at intervals because the light casings and electrical boxes lost their watertight integrity. To make matters worse, the *New York* strayed from course because her gyro compass malfunctioned. The malfunctioning compass required constant course corrections from the *Wyoming*.[19]

After the storm, the *Florida* managed to rejoin the division, but the *Delaware* sailed alone until meeting the British light cruiser *Constance* at the appointed rendezvous off the aptly named Cape Wrath at the northwest tip of Scotland at 0215 on 6 December. At 0200 the following day, the other battleships reached the rendezvous point. The *Manley* could not rejoin the division because she ran short on fuel and had to sail directly to her ultimate destination, the U.S. destroyer base at Queenstown, Ireland.[20]

At 1200 on 7 December 1917, Battleship Division Nine of the U.S. Navy steamed into the British Grand Fleet base at Scapa Flow. The sound of band music and cheering greeted the Americans as they berthed near the British men-of-war. Standing aft on his flagship, the *Queen Elizabeth*, Admiral Beatty, commander in chief of the Grand Fleet, raised his hat in a gesture of salute. The camouflaged American ships looked strangely out of place among the gray hulls of the British ships. The newcomers also showed the scars of their stormy passage across the North Atlantic. On the upper deck of the *Wyoming* was the wreckage of her two fifty-foot motor launches. Empty davits revealed where lifeboats had been. The other ships of the division were in similar condition.[21]

Admiral Rodman promptly paid a call on Admiral Beatty. The treacherous waters of Scapa Flow forced the American admiral to employ a British trawler instead of a ship's boat to reach Beatty's flagship. Rodman offered Beatty the services of himself, his ships, and his men. Beatty accepted, declaring, "Today marks an epoch in the history of England and America!"[22] In stark contrast to the rigid discipline and protocol of most British officers, Rodman reportedly remarked to Beatty, "I don't believe much in paper work. Whenever you have anything to bring to my attention, come and see me." Bemused, Beatty replied, "I'll do just that, Admiral."[23] The American dreadnoughts thereupon officially became the Sixth Battle Squadron of the Grand Fleet.[24]

The U.S. dreadnoughts added significantly to the Grand Fleet's strength. The American squadron constituted 12 percent of the British Grand Fleet and one-fourth of America's modern battleships.[25] Wartime oil shortages in England had necessitated that the U.S. Navy send coal-burning dreadnoughts instead of the newer, oil-fueled battleships, but the coal-burners were far from obsolete. With the exception of the new *Queen Elizabeth* and *Revenge* classes, Britain's battleships were also coal-burners, and the American battleships were comparable to their British coal-burning counterparts in terms of speed and armament.[26] Furthermore, the Grand Fleet had been on a war footing for over three years, and periods of long overhaul and engine maintenance had been out of the question. Many capital ships of the Grand Fleet could no longer make their contracted speed, and several could achieve only eighteen knots. The arrival of the American ships would allow more regular maintenance of British capital ships.

The oldest ship in the American squadron, the *Delaware*, was laid down in 1907 and carried ten 12-inch/45 caliber guns. She was a very successful ship. Capable of 21 knots, *Delaware* was slightly faster than the newer, oil-fueled *Nevada*-class battleships. The *Florida* class, authorized in 1908 and completed in 1911, was essentially a replica of the *Delaware* class, but with larger machinery spaces to accommodate four-shaft Parsons turbines—the same turbines used in British dreadnoughts. The *Wyoming*-class ships were considerably larger than the *Florida*s, with over 4,000 tons greater displacement. The *Wyoming*s carried twelve 12-inch/50 caliber guns.

Authorized in 1910 and completed in the spring of 1914, the *New York* class carried the new 14-inch/45 caliber guns. They reverted to the use of reciprocating engines because turbines did not provide sufficient range to steam from the West Coast to the Philippines in the event of war with Japan. The *New York*–class ships were the last coal-burning dreadnoughts built for the U.S. Navy.[27]

*

The Sixth Battle Squadron immediately began the difficult task of integrating itself into the British fleet. Admiral Rodman's willingness to adopt British methods and to take battle orders directly from Admiral Beatty was largely responsible for the ease with which the American squadron was assimilated. Rodman understood that two independent commands in one force simply would not work. Rodman also acknowledged that the British had actual war experience, which the Americans did not. He realized that, tactically, there was a great deal to learn from the British.[28]

British signals, radio codes, maneuvering orders, fire control methods, and battle instructions were all entirely new. When Division Nine first arrived in European waters, signals between British and American ships were in U.S. naval code. The Admiralty had provided a few copies of the *United States General Signal Book* to the Grand Fleet prior to the arrival of the Americans.[29] The Americans had studied the general British signal code while crossing the Atlantic, but could not yet use it proficiently. The American ships did not receive complete British signal books until after their arrival at Scapa Flow. The signal books included much information the Americans needed to learn, including the use of new ciphers, instructions for distribution of naval intelligence, instructions for entry into defended ports, and information on swept channels.[30] The Americans were impressed with the simplicity of the British visual signals, and the U.S. Navy adopted the British system after the war.[31]

The Grand Fleet operated according to an elaborate set of battle orders. Before 1918, these orders had been in two sections: "Grand Fleet Battle Instructions," which laid down tactical principles and guidelines, and "Grand Fleet Battle Orders," which were detailed instructions that amplified the battle instructions. On 1 January 1918 the battle orders became two separate series: "Grand Fleet Battle Instructions," which dealt with battle only, and "Grand Fleet Maneuvering Orders," dealing with cruising formations and changes of disposition.[32]

The fleet normally cruised in columns of squadrons abreast, but in battle would reorient itself 90 degrees to form a battle line. The divisions on the wing, or flank, of the fleet therefore had the farthest to travel to deploy for battle. Admiral Beatty assigned the Sixth Battle Squadron to be one of the fast divisions on the wing. In battle formation, the Fifth Battle Squadron, the other fast division, would take station at the van, and the Sixth Battle Squadron at the rear of the main battle line. In the event the fleet had to reorient itself quickly in the opposite direction using a "turnabout" maneuver, the Sixth Battle Squadron would become the van and the Fifth Squadron the rear of the battle line. The duty of the van division, besides engaging the enemy van, was to deny enemy light craft a favorable position from which to attack the main fleet with torpedoes and to engage enemy battle cruisers if British battle cruisers were absent. The duty of the rear division was to engage the rear squadron of the enemy line.[33]

In the event the enemy turned away under the cover of smoke and torpedo attack, as at Jutland, Beatty intended to accept the torpedo menace if necessary to keep the enemy from escaping. After the signal "Engage the enemy more closely," the fleet would concentrate on the rear of the enemy battle line. In this situation, Beatty instructed the rear squadron to press the enemy rear while the van squadron contained the enemy van. Beatty warned that the rear squadron would "necessarily come within torpedo range of the enemy and should therefore be in open order, ships being on a line at right angles to the enemy rear." This would allow the rear squadron to present a smaller target to torpedoes than if they maintained line ahead, which would present a broadside target. The rear squadron would use their secondary armament to break up the enemy destroyer flotillas retiring from their attack on the main British line.[34]

The Americans were proud of their position in the British battle line. Beatty assigned them their position because of the good condition and speed of the American ships. Their position would only have special importance if they became the van in a turnabout and led the British fleet into battle, but that was at least a remote possibility. Beatty did not assign the Americans their position because the rear squadron could come within torpedo range in battle and he did not wish to place British ships there. The rear squadron would not encounter any greater danger from torpedoes than the van squadron faced.[35]

The Sixth Battle Squadron had scarcely finished coaling when the entire fleet put to sea for maneuvers. Coaling the American ships, and cleaning up the mess, took nearly three days. The voyage across the Atlantic had nearly exhausted their coal supplies, and the small size of the British colliers made the coaling process especially slow.

The American squadron's first cruise into the North Sea with the Grand Fleet was a learning experience. The American lookouts had to learn to distinguish between flotsam and submarine periscopes. Captain Wiley, commander of *Wyoming*, recalled, "New ships arriving in the war zone usually did a good deal of shooting at submarines which were not submarines. With experience, they saw fewer."[36] Despite having had little time to learn, the Sixth Battle Squadron did manage to use the British code and was able to conform to maneuvers.[37]

On 17 December, with Christmas approaching, the Sixth Battle Squadron accompanied the *Queen Elizabeth* and *Iron Duke* to Rosyth, Britain's newest dockyard and base of the battle cruiser fleet, near Edinburgh on the Firth of Forth. Beatty's flagship needed an overhaul, and the *Iron Duke* acted as standby flagship. The American squadron used the opportunity to exercise in British maneuvers and signaling.

Royal Navy signalmen and telegraphists were lent to the ships of the Sixth Battle Squadron to teach British methods. The British sailors did not appreciate the spirit of democracy on the American ships, however. Royal Navy signals yeomen and petty officer telegraphists resented being ranked with U.S. Navy first class petty officers, who were younger and messed with the enlisted men. Beatty reported to the Admiralty that this system caused the British seamen "great dissatisfaction and discomfort." In the interest of avoiding disciplinary problems, Beatty requested that the Admiralty grant the signalmen and telegraphists the temporary rank of chief petty officer, which would allow them to take their meals in the chief petty officers' mess on the American ships. The Admiralty granted Beatty's request, and harmony returned.[38]

At Rosyth it was not all work and no play. Besides allowing time to gain knowledge of British methods, the Sixth Battle Squadron's stay at Rosyth allowed the Americans and British to become acquainted and to build camaraderie. The Americans were fortunate to enjoy liberty during the holiday season at Edinburgh rather than in the dreary Orkneys. The enlisted men of the *New York* hosted 125 poor or orphaned children on board for dinner and festivities. The people of Edinburgh greatly appreciated this act of good will. Many British officers invited their American counterparts to social gatherings and the local people were very hospitable.[39] The Sixth Battle Squadron finally left Rosyth for Scapa Flow along with the *Queen Elizabeth* and *Iron Duke* on 14 January, arriving the next morning.[40]

En route to Scapa Flow, the Sixth Battle Squadron engaged in full-caliber individual ship target practice in Pentland Firth. The practice was at long range (almost 12,000 yards) and was intended to simulate North Sea conditions. The results of this first practice firing came as a shock and a disappointment to the Americans and caused the British to doubt the proficiency of the American squadron.

During earlier full-caliber practices of three of the British battle squadrons in December 1917, the average rate of fire per salvo had been forty seconds or less, and the average spread was 300 to 500 yards. Among the American ships, only the *New York* managed the same rate of fire and spread, or pattern, of shot that the British ships consistently accomplished. The *New York* had average patterns of 464 yards and an average interval between salvos of 48 seconds.[41]

The *Delaware* had an acceptable average spread of 475 yards, but her rate of fire was a very slow 1 minute, 48 seconds. The most serious deficiency the practice revealed was the excessive salvo patterns of the *Wyoming* and the *Florida*. The *Wyoming*'s average spread per salvo was 956 yards; the *Florida*'s was a startling 1,131 yards! These excessive spreads were a serious handicap because dispersion of shot translates into fewer hits on the target.[42]

*

Admiral Beatty's assessment of the capability of the American squadron after the first six weeks was mixed. In a letter to King George V, Beatty reported that the Americans had worked very hard to become acquainted with British methods, but they were handicapped by their signaling and wireless equipment, which he considered very "primitive." Regarding their first gunnery practice, he stated that two ships did well and two badly. Beatty expressed concern over the excessive spread of the broadsides and the less-than-satisfactory rates of fire. He did note, however, that the Americans were working to correct the deficiencies.[43]

The king wrote to Admiral Beatty and expressed his pleasure that the United States squadron was fitting in. The king seemed to be defending the Americans when he wrote, "I expect they have a great deal to learn, but they will be a useful addition to your fleet."[44] He either minimized Beatty's concerns about the efficiency of the American ships or was anxious to avoid any political problems if Beatty failed to make the American squadron an integral part of the fleet.

In late January 1918, First Sea Lord Wemyss asked Admiral Beatty if he could detach three dreadnoughts to serve with the Dover Patrol, which protected a mine and net barrage across the straits of Dover. The Dover Patrol consisted of a force of trawlers and drifters tending the mine barrage, with a monitor and a few destroyers in support. German destroyers had attacked this force the previous spring, and future German raids were probable.[45] Wemyss noted that detaching units from the battle line would depend upon whether the American squadron was proficient enough to take their place.[46] Admiral Beatty replied that the American ships were coming along, but they were not yet the equivalent of British ships.[47]

The Grand Fleet, including the Sixth Battle Squadron, went to sea on 30 January for maneuvers in the North Sea. The Grand Fleet divided into two opposing forces. "Blue Fleet" comprised the three ships of the Fifth Battle Squadron, representing the First, Third, and Fourth Squadrons of the High Seas Fleet, with the Second Battle Cruiser Squadron in the van and several squadrons of light cruisers, two submarine flotillas, and destroyers in support. "Red Fleet" comprised the remainder of the battle fleet, with the First Battle Cruiser Squadron, four cruisers, four light cruisers, and destroyers in support.

As prearranged, the opposing fleets converged upon a point in the North Sea, roughly on the same latitude as Pentland Firth and midway between Scapa Flow and Norway. Once the opposing fleets made contact, Beatty directed the exercises by signal. These maneuvers were for practicing cruiser reports and deployments for battle.[48] Rodman reported to the Navy Department that his squadron experienced "not the slightest difficulty" in communications or conforming to deployments. He did mention that a German U-boat had upset one particular exercise. Two ships of the Fifth Battle Squadron, ahead of the *New York*, sighted the hostile submarine and one of them attempted to ram it while its conning tower was awash. Destroyers rushed to drop depth charges, but the submarine apparently escaped. After completing the maneuvers, the fleet returned to Scapa Flow on 2 February.[49]

In his weekly general report to Secretary Daniels, Rodman made a number of observations about the maneuvers. Regarding the responsibility of force commanders, Rodman reported, "Much more latitude is given these commanders than with us. They are made acquainted with the policy of the commander in chief, and conduct their commands with more freedom of action, and are entrusted with more responsibility." Rodman also noted that station keeping in the battle line was not as strict as in the U.S. fleet. This allowed individual ships the freedom to alter course one point on either side of the base course in order to confuse enemy range-taking during battle. In addition, he commented on the difficulty of operations in North Sea conditions. In particular, hazy weather conditions reduced visibility to the point that judging distances or taking accurate ranges with a rangefinder was extremely difficult.[50]

During the maneuvers, the American squadron evidently performed well enough to suit the commander in chief. The Americans did not, however, inspire Beatty's admiration and respect. Beatty expressed his opinion of the American squadron in a letter to his wife on 5 February: "The American squadron enjoyed themselves greatly while we were out, and did well, and will do better next time. I am sending old Rodman out on an operation of his own, which pleases him and gives them an idea that they are really taking part in the war. I trust they will come to no harm."[51]

*

The independent operation that Beatty gave Rodman's squadron was part of an ongoing operation to protect Scandinavian convoys from attack by German surface raiders. These convoys were important in ensuring continued Allied trade with Norway, Sweden, and Denmark. Without this trade, the Allies would lose important sources of iron ore, nitrates, and other chemicals.

In April 1917, the British had begun providing escorts of destroyers and armed trawlers for the Scandinavian convoys. These escorts gave adequate protection against U-boats, but in October 1917 a new threat had emerged.[52] German headquarters decided to assist the U-boat campaign with a surface attack on the Scandinavian trade. The Germans reasoned (accurately, as it turned out) that such an attack would force the Admiralty to provide better protection for the Scandinavian convoys, thus removing units from antisubmarine patrols.[53] The Germans chose the light cruisers *Brummer* and *Bremse* for the task because of their excellent speed (28 knots) and range. Both ships were designed as minelayers, and so carried only four 5.9-inch guns instead of the usual eight of other German light cruisers.[54]

At 0600 on 17 October, *Strongbow*, one of the escorting destroyers for the westbound Scandinavian convoy, sighted two strange ships approaching. Before the British destroyer could even come to action stations, 5.9-inch shell fire from *Bremmer* and *Bremse* reduced it to a sinking hulk. The German cruisers then proceeded to fire on *Strongbow*'s helpless survivors. The convoy's other escorting destroyer, *Mary Rose,* was cruising ahead of the convoy and heard the firing astern. Rushing to the scene, *Mary Rose* engaged the German cruisers in a desperate but futile attempt to save the convoy. *Mary Rose* suffered the same fate as *Strongbow,* and nine of the twelve freighters in the convoy were sunk.[55]

On 12 December, the Germans followed their October success with another raid. The German light cruiser *Emden* accompanied two half-flotillas of Germany's newest destroyers to the Dogger Bank. *Emden* remained behind while the two half-flotillas separated to hunt independently. At 0930, the Third Half Flotilla, consisting of four destroyers, sighted an eastbound Scandinavian convoy and engaged the two escorting destroyers, *Partridge* and *Pellew.* The British destroyers attempted to draw the enemy away from the convoy, leaving four armed trawlers to defend it. Three German destroyers followed and one remained to attack the convoy. Early in the action, the Germans sank *Partridge. Pellew* escaped in a rain squall, the only ship in the convoy to survive. The trawlers never stood a chance against the modern German destroyers. The Germans sank all five, plus the six freighters in the convoy.[56]

The disasters to the Scandinavian convoys had serious repercussions in Britain. The Admiralty's failure to protect the Scandinavian convoys precipitated Admiral Jellicoe's downfall as First Sea Lord and a reappraisal of Grand Fleet policy.[57] In November, the First Lord of the Admiralty told the House of Commons that it was the responsibility of the commander in chief of the Grand Fleet to safeguard the convoys. Consequently, Admiral Beatty felt obliged to detach a battleship division on a regular basis to cover the Scandinavian convoys.[58]

Beginning in January 1918, the battleships of the Grand Fleet engaged in the business of convoy escort. The submarine crisis had already forced the U.S. Navy to abandon its Mahanite policy of fleet concentration, and now the threat of surface raiders was forcing the Grand Fleet too to depart from this doctrine. Paul Halpern points out that detaching a division of the battle fleet to cover the convoys was a calculated risk, because it presented the Germans with the long sought-after possibility of concentrating overwhelming force against a portion of the Grand Fleet. To guard against this threat, the Admiralty became even more dependent on the ability of naval intelligence to detect German moves.[59]

✳

At around 2100 on Wednesday, 6 February, the Sixth Battle Squadron stood out from the east channel of Scapa Flow and set course for a North Sea rendezvous with an eastbound Scandinavian convoy. The American battleships with their screening destroyers were in company with the Third Light Cruiser Squadron and its screening destroyers. This force provided cover, or support, for the convoy and its own light escort. The entire covering force for operation "Z6" was under the command of Admiral Rodman. This was the first time that British men-of-war had ever served under an American admiral.[60]

Operational doctrine consisted of always remaining to the south, between the convoy and the German naval bases. The covering force would sight the convoy at daybreak, at some prearranged time during the day, and at dusk. Upon arrival near Norway, the covering force would cruise in an area to the south, waiting until a returning convoy was ready for the voyage to the British Isles.

Early on the morning of 7 February, Rodman's force picked up convoy "OZ6." There were around thirty ships in the convoy. Its light escort consisted of the armed auxiliary *Duke of Clarence* and eight or ten armed trawlers. The voyage to Norway was pleasant and uneventful. The convoy enjoyed excellent weather and good visibility, which is quite unusual for the North Sea in that season. The only excitement that first day was the sighting of a smoke shell descending in the southwest, presumably dropped from an aircraft to attract their attention, though the purpose may have been to indicate the position of other forces.[61]

Friday, 8 February, was a very eventful day. At daylight, as the ships neared Norwegian territorial waters, men on the battleships and one of the light cruisers heard firing from the northeast—at least four shots from a 4- or 5-inch gun. The battleships steamed in the direction of the firing, but failed to find anything. The source of the firing remains a mystery.[62]

The covering force then parted company with the eastbound convoy and remained outside of Norwegian territorial waters to wait for the return convoy "HZ7," which was sailing from Selbiorns Fiord. While maneuvering to the south of Stavanger, the battleships steamed in line abreast, in open order. At 1322 the *New York* hoisted a green submarine warning flag, but annulled it almost immediately when one of the screening destroyers, *Valorous*, reported porpoises. Less than five minutes later, however, the *Wyoming* again gave the signal and reported a submarine in sight. At about the same time, the *Florida* spotted a large wake, assumed to be a submerged submarine, crossing her bow from port to starboard about 500 yards ahead. She veered out of the line and crossed this wake in an unsuccessful attempt to ram the submarine. A destroyer followed in the *Florida*'s wake and dropped a depth charge.

A few minutes later, after straightening out her course, the *Florida*'s bridge and foretop spotters reported the turbulence of a torpedo that passed 100 yards abeam. At 1353 the officer in the spotting top of the *Delaware* also reported a torpedo, on the starboard bow crossing the ship's track. The *Delaware* turned hard to starboard and avoided the torpedo, which passed ahead of the ship by several hundred yards. The spotter then reported the wake of a periscope or another torpedo coming from the same direction as the first. With the disturbance steadied on the her port-quarter, the *Delaware* fired a 3-inch round that went over the mark by 200 yards at a range of 2,000 yards. About this time, one of the destroyers fired a depth charge at the wake.

The *Florida* and the *Delaware* had just regained position with the *New York* and the *Wyoming* when the *Florida* spotted yet another torpedo wake passing between the herself and the *Wyoming.* This wake passed ahead of the ships.

At 1408 the *Florida*'s maintop spotter sighted twin periscopes at a distance of 500 yards on the starboard beam, but they submerged before the *Florida*'s guns could bear. A few moments later, the foretop spotter sighted another torpedo passing astern from the general direction of the periscope sighting. Meanwhile, the *Delaware*'s lookout spotted a torpedo wake dead ahead. The *Delaware* turned hard to port and passed just inside of the wake.

En route to rejoin the squadron, the *Delaware* sighted suspicious objects floating 800 yards off the port beam and directed the destroyers to investigate. The destroyers investigated and reported finding fishermen's floats.[63]

The remainder of the voyage was without mishap. The covering force left the westbound convoy at 1730 on 9 February and proceeded to Scapa Flow, arriving at around 0400 the next day.[64]

Captain Wiley of the *Wyoming* was never convinced that any submarines really existed that day. His lookouts never saw the torpedoes that the *Florida* and the *Delaware* reported. In his memoir, Wiley recalled, "I think probably the first alarm was caused by a porpoise, which, bobbing up and down, might easily look to a newcomer like the conning tower of a submarine. However that may be, and serious as it was at the time, when we got settled down I thought I would split with laughing."[65]

Rodman, on the other hand, was convinced that U-boats had attacked his ships that day. He wrote letters of commendation for Captain Scales of the *Delaware* and Captain Washington of the *Florida* for the skillful handling of their ships during the torpedo attack. In his weekly report, Rodman reported that two torpedoes were fired at the *Florida* and two at the *Delaware*. He further stated, "These vessels owe their safety to their vigilance, prompt and skillful maneuvering." In his report to Beatty, Rodman also praised the skillful and efficient handling of the destroyers. Neither Rodman, nor Beatty, nor the Navy Department appear to have questioned the validity of the submarine sightings.[66]

Based on subsequent analysis, Wiley was apparently correct in believing that frolicking porpoises were the cause of the alarm. Two German submarines, U-80 and U-82, were in the vicinity, but neither sighted any warships nor made any attacks that day.[67]

*

The day after the Americans returned from convoy duty, the *Texas*, sister ship of the *New York*, joined the Sixth Battle Squadron. The *Texas* was under the command of Capt. Victor Blue, formerly the chief of the Bureau of Navigation.

Not long after joining the Grand Fleet, Rodman had requested that the Navy Department send an additional battleship to join the Sixth Battle Squadron. He explained that this would allow the American ships to conform to British organization. The Grand Fleet always maintained a high state of readiness, with all ships continually on four hours' notice to put to sea, and frequently at one and one-half hours' notice. Without regular refits, the ships could not maintain this state of readiness, so the British kept an extra ship in each squadron to use as a substitute when any ship in the squadron required repairs. In this way, each squadron retained its strength even when one ship was absent for an overhaul.[68]

After Rodman made the request for the addition of the *Texas*, both Benson and Sims conferred with the Admiralty about instead relieving the entire division sometime during the summer of 1918 to return to the United States for overhaul, replacing it with another division. The Admiralty agreed, pointing out the lack of labor and repair facilities in Britain. Furthermore, the British expressed their belief that more than one U.S. battleship division could eventually operate in European waters. The Admiralty seemed confident that Norway would eventually enter the war and hoped that a major fleet base in Norway would become available to the Allies. The addition of a Norwegian base would provide the facilities to support a larger part of the U.S. fleet.[69]

In early January 1918, Sims apparently resubmitted Rodman's request that the *Texas* join the Sixth Battle Squadron. Benson informed Sims that the department did not consider a five-ship division desirable because it was counter to U.S. battleship organization. The department could send another battleship, but only if a real need existed. Benson reiterated that the department would prefer to send another complete four-ship division to the Grand Fleet, if the supply situation were adequate, rather than alter its organization.[70]

Sims responded by pointing out the need for another ship with 14-inch guns at the American end of the battle line. Without one, if the *New York* required repairs, there would be no ship with 14-inch guns in the squadron and, until the *New York* returned, the Sixth Battle Squadron would be undergunned. He explained that there was no room for the Navy Department to send an entire additional U.S. battleship division, because it would place too great a strain on British supply and repair facilities.

Sims also reported that the Admiralty had reversed its earlier position about relieving Rodman's division to return to the United States for overhaul. After consulting with Beatty, the Admiralty had agreed that it was better for Division Nine to remain with the fleet, rather than having another division replace it. The Admiralty considered that the time needed to train another division in British methods was not worth the benefit of not having the burden of refitting the American ships.[71] Sims's arguments apparently convinced the Navy Department. The *Texas* began preparations for service overseas on 19 January, and sailed for Scapa Flow on 30 January.[72]

The *Texas* had recently completed repairs of damage from an unfortunate encounter with Block Island on Long Island Sound. Captain Blue and his navigator, confused about shore lights and more concerned about the minefield at the opening of the sound, made the turn at the wrong time and ran the ship aground on the island from the bow all the way aft beyond midships. Captain Blue, a protégé of Secretary Daniels, was never court-martialed and remained in command of the *Texas*. The Navy Department held the navigator entirely responsible for the accident.[73]

At the end of February, Admiral Rodman requested another change in the composition of the Sixth Battle Squadron. He admitted that his division now had enough ships to carry out its mission, but explained that the American battleships still could not conform to Grand Fleet policy. The practice of the Grand Fleet was to concentrate the fire of two or more ships on one of the enemy's ships, as shown in the accompanying figure. The concentrated fire had to be of the same caliber for spotting purposes. He considered that the position of the Sixth Battle Squadron at the rear or van of the battle line made it especially important to follow the British method of fire concentration.[74]

Rodman suggested that, if possible, all of his ships should be of the same caliber and muzzle velocity. The ideal squadron would comprise the *New York*, *Texas*, *Oklahoma*, and *Nevada*—all of the same size and gun-caliber—with the *Wyoming* as a spare. However, recognizing that the oil shortage would probably preclude the participation of the oil-burning *Oklahoma* and *Nevada*, Rodman proposed that in that case the *Arkansas*, sister ship of the *Wyoming*, should replace the *Delaware*, leaving the *Florida* as a spare. This disposition would give the squadron two pairs of ships with the same caliber and range. It would also alleviate the problem caused by the limited range of the *Delaware*'s and the *Florida*'s guns. Neither ship's guns had a range of over 19,000 yards, after the ballistic correction for colder temperatures was taken into account, and Grand Fleet policy discouraged a fighting range of less than 16,000 yards because of the danger of torpedoes. Therefore, the two ships could not engage at the extreme ranges of the other ships. In addition, Rodman asked that the department not send either the *North Dakota* or the *Utah* because in his opinion they had unreliable engines.

The admiral admitted he was "in the dark" about intentions to increase the battleship force serving in European waters with another division. He urged that if the Navy Department contemplated such a move, "then the sooner the better," because it would take a month to six weeks to break-in another ship.[75]

A British liaison officer to the Sixth Battle Squadron, Capt. H. E. F. Aylmer, forwarded a copy of Rodman's memorandum to Beatty via the captain of the fleet. Aylmer reported the rumor that more ships could join the American squadron. He spoke in favor of the *Arkansas*'s replacement of the *Delaware* and noted that the *Florida*, although armed with the same caliber of guns, had greater elevation and therefore greater range than *Delaware*. Aylmer also mentioned that the principal factor governing the time required to train new ships was the training of wireless/telegraph operators. He stated that all other departments of the American ships learned British methods rapidly, but even the best wireless operators needed at least two months' experience before gaining sufficient competence.[76]

In a cable to Benson, Sims supported Rodman's request for the addition of the *Arkansas* to the Sixth Battle Squadron. He did not, however, support the idea of sending any oil-burners, because of the short supply

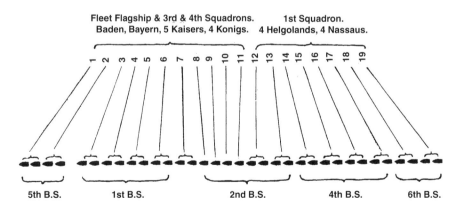

Diagram of the normal distribution of fire for the Grand Fleet. Targets were assigned by battle squadron in the British fleet to avoid concentrating the fire on only a few targets and leaving the rest of the enemy line untouched. The American squadron was designated the Sixth Battle Squadron. The U.S. Atlantic Fleet adopted a similar system of fleet concentration after the war. *Adapted from "Grand Fleet Battle Instructions," 1 January 1918, ADM 116/1342, Public Record Office.*

of oil in Britain. Sims reiterated Rodman's arguments and suggested that the *Arkansas* be fitted with paravanes that had heavier underwater castings and fittings before her departure. Paravanes were devices invented during World War I as a defense against moored mines. When the bow wave of a ship pushed a mine aside, the mooring wire would be deflected onto the tow wire of the paravane and into a wirecutter. The detached mine would then float to the surface where it could be destroyed by rifle fire. Heavier paravane fittings were needed because the fittings the Navy Department had earlier provided to the Sixth Battle Squadron had proven to be inadequate in North Sea conditions.[77]

Sims followed up the next day with a memorandum to Navy Secretary Daniels. He maintained that the Grand Fleet policy of concentrating fire by pairs was very practical. Recent experimental firing with *Marlborough* and *Iron Duke* had proven its efficacy. Sims explained that concentrated fire from pairs of ships with the same gun-caliber, range, and muzzle velocity greatly facilitated the exchange and combination of fire control data.[78]

Despite the advice of Sims and Rodman, however, the Navy Department decided not to dispatch *Arkansas* for service with the American squadron at that time.[79]

*

On 16 February at 0100, the Grand Fleet, including the Sixth Battle Squadron, sailed to reinforce the Fourth Battle Squadron, which was supporting a Scandinavian convoy. Naval intelligence indicated that the German battle cruisers had sortied, and Beatty hoped to intercept them. The operation took place during a severe gale. Because of the importance of the mission, all ships held their course despite the heavy weather, and were thus prevented from maneuvering to lessen the effects of the storm.[80] Sometime after 0330, heavy seas damaged the *Delaware*'s steamer, a sailer, and two whaleboats. The starboard gangway ladder and gratings were destroyed and there was considerable damage to the ventilators. Later, the *Delaware* developed more serious problems. Without warning, the dynamos stopped, cutting off all electrical power. Engine room blowers stopped, forcing the ship to reduce speed to 12 knots. Most of the ship fell into darkness and communications were limited to voice tubes for half an hour, until the dynamos were repaired and normal conditions resumed. The cause of the power failure had been a small amount of water that leaked through a voice tube into the dynamos. The power failure was a great inconvenience at the time, but in battle it could have been fatal.[81]

During this operation, the fleet suffered more than just material loss. Heavy seas washed a sailor overboard from the *New York*, and he was lost. In addition, the British ships lost a sublieutenant and ten or twelve men to the sea.[82] Admiral Rodman recalled the difficulty of making no attempt to save a man washed overboard, but had to weigh "the balance against stopping, losing time and position, whereby the main force might lose strength in case of an engagement, or when slowing down might cause the loss of the ship by an attack of a hostile submarine."[83] The operation must have been frustrating for all concerned. The fleet failed to find the German battle cruisers, and so turned back for Scapa Flow at 1400. High winds and heavy seas continued to batter the fleet until it reached the shelter of land. At midnight the American squadron proceeded through Hoxa Sound to its anchorage.[84]

During late February the Sixth Battle Squadron carried out several target practices, with continuing disappointing results. The squadron, less the *New York*, which was refitting, exercised at torpedo defense on 19 February. This involved the secondary battery of 5-inch guns. Also on the same day, the *Texas* carried out individual full-caliber firings with reduced charges. Rodman reported that their shooting was "not up to the standard of excellence that would be expected from ships which had made such fine records during the past year." He listed such reasons for the unsatisfactory performance as the large turnover in personnel and the fact that the exercises were carried out in actual war conditions. Practices with the Atlantic Fleet were held in favorable conditions and on a course with a previously determined range.[85] Rodman later commented on the performance of the *Texas:* "In spite of her four years commission, that she has now the gunnery trophy, and was flying the efficiency pennant, *she was not ready to fire under war conditions.*" Rodman felt that the poor performance of the *Texas* and the other ships in his division was a commentary on the U.S. system of gunnery practice, which emphasized a good score over actual war readiness.[86]

The efficacy of the American battleships came up during a conference between Admiral Beatty and Rear Adm. Sidney Fremantle, the deputy chief of naval staff. The Admiralty was concerned about the possibility that the Germans would conduct a naval offensive in the English Channel as a means of protecting their right flank when the western land offensive resumed. The Admiralty hoped that Beatty could release three *Superb*-class battleships from the Grand Fleet to reinforce the Third Battle Squadron, which then consisted of *Dreadnought*, a *King Edward VII*–class pre-dreadnought, and an old light cruiser.

Beatty argued against detaching any capital ships from the fleet. He pointed out that having to protect the Norwegian convoys required continually keeping at least a division, and sometimes an entire squadron, at sea. Additionally, a battleship division was continually refitting. Furthermore, Beatty considered that the Grand Fleet must begin any battle with a large superiority of forces because losses, presumably to destroyer and submarine ambushes, had to be expected. He added that if the danger of a German offensive was great, then the Admiralty should bring the entire Grand Fleet further south to Rosyth and possibly station an advance force on the Humber. However, Beatty pointed out the added problems in fleet concentration if the Grand Fleet moved from Scapa Flow.

When Admiral Fremantle inquired about the efficiency of the American battleships, Beatty replied that the Admiralty still could not consider them the equivalent of a British battle squadron. He felt that their tactical efficiency was fine and that they were learning rapidly, but their gunnery was "distinctly poor and disappointing," although he expressed faith that they would improve. Besides, he added, the Americans were stationed in a position of the battle line where they were unlikely to interfere with the movements of the fleet.[87]

In late March 1918, First Sea Lord Wemyss again pressured Admiral Beatty to release three dreadnoughts from the Grand Fleet. He was concerned about the possibility of a raid on the east coast of England and the need to reinforce the Dover Patrol. Beatty contended that the U.S. dreadnoughts did not yet have enough wartime experience to replace British fighting units, even after four months in the war zone. Wemyss replied, "I would not think of pressing you to reduce your force to anything smaller than you think is absolutely necessary. It is, of course, a great disappointment that the Americans are not coming along quickly enough."[88]

Beatty was always careful to conceal these thoughts from the Americans. He evidently did not want to harm the morale of the Sixth Battle Squadron or jeopardize his working relationship with Admiral Rodman.[89] Nevertheless, many American officers felt inferior in the company of their British counterparts. Captain Wiley of the *Wyoming* remembered, "We were all green, in new and swift company. I wanted everything to go well. We were under scrutiny."[90]

Admiral Rodman was especially heavy-handed in his efforts to live up to the British standard. On one occasion during maneuvers, the *Texas* was attempting to take in her paravanes when they got snarled up and she had to drop out of formation. Rodman ordered the other ships to close up and then reverse order of formation. In the process, the *Wyoming* overran its position and ran up on the *New York*. The admiral was so furious that he used the signals to curse Captain Wiley and the *Wyoming* in plain view of the rest of the fleet. Upon returning to Scapa Flow, Wiley went aboard the flagship and told the admiral that if such humiliation was necessary, then Rodman should replace him with another captain. Rodman softened and said that he was so filled with ambition that it made him harsher than he realized. He explained that he was not ambitious for his own benefit, but he did not want to have a squadron that was inferior to any British squadron.[91]

✳

The Sixth Battle Squadron, with a screen of eight destroyers, put to sea again at 2330 on 8 March to provide cover for another Scandinavian convoy. At 0715 the next morning, the battleships rendezvoused with convoy "OZ15," again with the auxiliary steamer *Duke of Clarence* and two destroyers as an escort. The Second Light Cruiser Squadron from Rosyth, consisting of the *Sydney, Dublin, Southampton, Melbourne, Birmingham*, and four destroyers of the 13th Flotilla also joined the covering force at that time.[92] Unlike the Americans' first convoy duty, the weather was very heavy, and progress was slow.

The next evening, six hours behind schedule, the convoy proceeded alone for the final thirty-five miles to Stavanger. Rodman received word that the return convoy would meet them at 0900 the next morning, the eleventh. Because there was heavy fog that night, Rodman assigned courses and speeds for the night and scheduled a rendezvous for 0600.[93]

About half an hour before reaching the morning rendezvous, the *New York* hoisted a signal flag ordering a change of course to avoid a thick fog bank that lay ahead. The result was very nearly a catastrophe. The fog closed in before all of the other ships could receive and acknowledge the change of course. In the following confusion, ships of the Sixth Battle Squadron and the light cruiser squadron narrowly escaped collision. Rodman credited the quick and efficient handling of the individual ships with saving the day.

The day was not over, however, nor had the fog lifted. A radio signal went out to order the entire force to steer west, but the *Texas, Florida,* and *Wyoming,* along with four destroyers, failed to receive it and became separated from the rest of the force. As the weather began to clear, the light cruiser squadron scouted for, and found, the convoy. The visibility continued to be poor, however, and the missing battleships could not rejoin the force until the next morning. Nor was fog the only hazard. Both the *Florida* and the *Delaware* reported periscope sightings, and the force received two radio reports that warned of U-boats in the area that had been detected by direction-finding stations. In addition, a floating mine was destroyed by gunfire. The Sixth Battle Squadron finally returned to Scapa Flow at 1730 on Tuesday, 13 March.[94]

Two days after the American battleships returned from convoy duty, the chief of naval operations cabled Admiral Sims to express concern over the Admiralty's policy of using modern battleships to escort the Norwegian convoys. Benson emphasized that he did not want to spare the American squadron any of the risks that other ships in the Grand Fleet faced, but he could not understand how and why the British would utilize battleships in a way that was "so contrary to our present conception of the general strategy of the Grand Fleet and reason for its being." Benson noted that the practice also departed from the "fleet-in-being" doctrine that guided U.S. naval strategy, whose goal was to engage the enemy battle fleet. He asked if the risk was actually worth the gain and if the Allied superiority in dreadnoughts warranted the risk. Would it not be wiser, he inquired, to use obsolete battleships for the task? Benson conceded that the greater speed and better compartmentalization of dreadnoughts was perhaps sufficient reason for using them, but he stated that if a shortage of ships was the reason for using them, then the department would rather send less valuable pre-dreadnoughts into the war zone for that duty.[95] Benson was correct in observing that the use of dreadnoughts as escorts was a radical departure from both U.S. and British naval doctrine, and his concern for the safety of battleships operating so far from the support of the fleet was certainly justified.

Sims replied to Benson, defending the Admiralty's position as usual, and insisting that the use of dreadnoughts was the only way to safeguard the Norwegian convoys against surface attack. He maintained that the convoys were important enough to incur some risks to the capital ships. Sims seemed to have great faith in British naval intelligence, and tried to calm Benson by assuring him that the fleet always reinforced the battleship escort when there was knowledge of enemy forces operating in Heligoland Bight. Sims recommended that the department not send pre-dreadnoughts for the duty because they were more vulnerable than modern ships and the additional shipping needed for their supply would be prohibitive. Sims's reply evidently satisfied Benson, because the Navy Department did not take the matter any further.[96]

In mid-April, the Grand Fleet, including the American squadron, moved to its new fleet anchorage at Rosyth. The move south put the Grand Fleet in a more favorable position strategically. On Wednesday, 17 April, the Sixth Battle Squadron sailed on what would prove to be their last mission to protect the Scandinavian convoys. At 0900 the battleships proceeded out of the Firth of Forth in company with their screen, which included the flotilla leader *Parker* and five "R"-class destroyers. The *Delaware* was in dry dock for repairs and installation of paravane gear, and so did not join the squadron for the mission. The Fourth Light Cruiser Squadron, including the *Calliope*, *Cambrian*, and *Caroline*, had already joined convoy "OZ25" when the battleships left Rosyth.[97]

Not long after leaving the anchorage, the *Texas* reported sighting a periscope and opened fire. Two of the destroyers quickly dropped several depth charges, with no apparent success. The destroyers could not have hit the submarine because once again, none was present; the *Texas* was shooting at a phantom.[98]

Before long, however, a more tangible enemy—the sea—rose against the squadron and its small escorts. During that first night at sea, a gale hit with such strong seas that the force had to slow for the safety of the destroyers. The gale continued through the eighteenth, and progress was very slow. Progress was also slow for the convoy. When the battleship force finally sighted the first stragglers at daylight on Friday, 19 April, the convoy stretched sixty miles in length and was twenty-four hours behind schedule.

The return convoy sailed at noon that day, just as the gale was beginning to blow itself out. The Sixth Battle Squadron accompanied the convoy until 2000, when the commander in chief ordered them by signal to return to Rosyth. The Americans arrived there at 1625 on 20 April.[99]

*

These Scandinavian convoys, and their covering force of first-rate battleships, were too attractive a target for the German Staff to pass up indefinitely. In the opinion of the commander in chief of the High Seas Fleet, Adm. Reinhard Scheer, "A successful attack on such a convoy would not only result in the sinking of much tonnage, but would be a great military success, and would bring welcome relief to the U-boats operating in the Channel and round England." He felt strongly enough about it to commit the entire battle fleet against a Scandinavian convoy. At 0600 on 23 April, Scheer's battle squadrons sailed on what would be the last sortie of the High Seas Fleet.[100]

The Germans took elaborate measures and observed strict radio silence to avoid detection. In spite of this, a British submarine, the J.6, sighted the German fleet as it proceeded out of Heligoland Bight, but she failed to make a report because her commander believed he had sighted British cruisers, which were expected to be in the area supporting a British minelaying operation. Thus, on the morning of Wednesday, 24 April, the High Seas Fleet approached the Norwegian coast unreported.

The failure of British naval intelligence would have ensured the success of the German raid, if inaccurate German intelligence had not doomed the operation from the beginning. U-boat reports had led Scheer to believe that the convoys sailed every three days, but the Admiralty had recently changed the schedule of sailings to every four days. The next convoy was not due to leave England until that day. In the words of Henry Newbolt, "Admiral Scheer and his battle squadrons were steaming into a no-man's sea, abandoned alike by merchantmen and men-of-war."[101]

As German battle cruisers searched for the nonexistent convoy, the battle cruiser *Moltke* lost a screw, which caused the turbine to race and a wheel to explode. Fragments pierced the discharge pipe of a condenser, and the central engine room flooded. She took on 2,000 tons of water, putting the center and starboard engines out of commission. *Moltke* attempted to close with the main fleet, but her condition deteriorated and she was forced to break radio silence to ask assistance from the fleet. From this transmission, the British finally learned that German capital ships were loose in the North Sea.[102]

The Grand Fleet, including the Sixth Battle Squadron less *Wyoming*, sailed to intercept the High Seas Fleet at 1500 on 24 April.[103] Meanwhile, the German fleet had turned for home with *Moltke* in tow. The German fleet remained in company with the crippled *Moltke*, and so had to reduce speed to 10–11 knots.[104] Nevertheless, Scheer managed to evade the Grand Fleet.

At 1000 on the twenty-fifth, vessels of the Grand Fleet's advance screen made contact with the enemy fleet, but no action followed. The High Seas Fleet returned to the safety of its defenses, and so ended the last opportunity to bring the German fleet to battle.[105]

At one point during the Grand Fleet's chase of the High Seas Fleet, the Germans reversed course. This required the Grand Fleet to come about, putting the Sixth Battle Squadron in the van. Had the Grand Fleet overhauled the Germans, the American ships would have led the British fleet into what might have turned out to be the decisive naval battle of the war. After returning to port, several British admirals referred to the American position in the line and expressed their confidence and congratulations for what might have been.[106]

It is interesting to speculate about what could have happened as a result of the last sortie of the High Seas Fleet. Admiral Beatty narrowly missed intercepting Scheer, which could have resulted in a decisive victory against the German fleet. Marder points out that Scheer took a serious risk in visiting northern waters because he was unaware that the Grand Fleet had moved south to Rosyth, on his flank.[107]

The last sortie could as easily have ended in disaster to the Scandinavian convoy and its covering force. Beatty had warned the Admiralty of the grave risks to the Scandinavian convoys' covering force should the German fleet escape into the North Sea undetected.[108] The last sortie of the

German fleet justified Beatty's concerns and highlighted the vulnerability of the covering force and the limitations of British naval intelligence.

The American squadron had been the covering force for the Scandinavian convoy of 17–19 April, and therefore had missed Scheer's sortie by less than a week. Commenting on this fact, Paul Halpern contemplates how easily they could have met with disaster: "The service of the American battleships with the Grand Fleet has traditionally been treated as a rather ho-hum affair, dull but necessary. One wonders about the effect on American public opinion had those battleships fallen in with the High Seas Fleet with a loss of three or four ships and a few thousand lives."[109] The American battleships certainly were in harm's way, and their service in the war zone deserves more than the footnote of recognition they have received.

*

The sortie of the High Seas Fleet against the Norwegian convoy caused Admiral Rodman to doubt the wisdom of using valuable capital ships as a covering force. In his general report of 27 April, Rodman called attention to the plan of operations requiring the supporting force of battleships to remain at a dangerous distance from the Grand Fleet's base for a few days at a time, inviting an enemy attack in force. Rodman perceived that the safety of the covering force depended entirely upon the naval intelligence of the opposing forces—Beatty's knowledge of German fleet movements and the German ability to predict the timing of the convoys. Furthermore, he believed that he was not the only one with misgivings: "I am of the opinion, which is shared by most, if not all of the flag officers of the Grand Fleet, that there are possibilities of a grave disaster to the supporting force, and that it is a matter for deep consideration."[110]

Rodman's report passed first to the force commander, Admiral Sims. Sims was alarmed that Rodman's criticism would become known and damage relations with the commander in chief and the Admiralty. He returned it, suggesting that Rodman remove all the critical references. In a personal letter, Sims sternly rebuked Rodman and completely dismissed his concerns:

> The criticism in question is far from slight. It amounts to an expression of practically complete lack of confidence in the ability of the Commander-in-Chief and the Admiralty to handle the fleet with safety to its detachments—

an opinion, moreover, that is necessarily based upon a portion only of the information wholly necessary to form a correct opinion. It is not necessary for me to supply this information or to discuss the matter beyond assuring you that the dispositions which you criticize were thoroughly considered by the Admiralty in connection with continuous information from scouting forces not belonging to the Grand Fleet, and information from other sources, and that the danger which you have assumed has not at any time existed.[111]

Sims sent a copy of his letter to Benson and explained that "Rodman has been doing excellent work with the fleet but he is rather impulsive and liable to 'slop over' at times." Sims added that Rodman probably did not consider how detrimental his criticisms would be, and that there would probably not be any more trouble out of him.[112] As Sims predicted, Rodman was careful to hold his peace after the rebuke from the force commander.[113] Besides, Rodman's concern soon became moot when the British reduced the covering force to only a light cruiser squadron in June 1918, and to a pair of armored cruisers later.[114]

The Sixth Battle Squadron's involvement in protecting the Scandinavian convoys also made an issue of Rodman's rank and caused another of the many disagreements between Sims and the Navy Department. In early February, Beatty requested that the Admiralty arrange for Rodman's advancement from rear admiral to vice admiral. During escort duty, Rodman's squadron worked with a light cruiser squadron. Beatty wanted the flag officer in charge of the battle squadron to command the force, but because British practice in granting rank differed from the rank structure in the U.S. Navy, Rodman was junior to all of the other flag officers commanding battle squadrons and even to some commanding light cruiser squadrons. Beatty made it clear that Rodman was "an officer of high attainments and . . . eminently suitable for the rank." He did not want Rodman replaced with an American vice admiral, but wanted Rodman advanced.[115]

Sims supported the proposal to advance Rodman in rank. In a letter of congratulation, he expressed his gratification that Rodman had made such a fine impression on the British. Interestingly, Sims told Rodman that he had taken pains to ensure Benson that the idea had originated with the British, lest the Navy Department suspect that Sims championed Rodman's advancement as a way to advance his own.[116]

Sims's congratulations were premature. In late April, when the Navy

Department finally acted on the request, Sims had to write Rodman a letter of condolence: "I am very sorry that the Department has not seen fit to favor this proposition, as it seemed to me that it should be done out of consideration of not only the conditions that pertain in the Grand Fleet, but out of all consideration for the request of our principal ally."[117]

The refusal to grant Rodman's advancement evidently came directly from President Wilson, who was very jealous of U.S. independence and resented Admiralty interference in U.S. practices.[118] The president did not want U.S. officers to become too associated with British organization and methods. For this same reason the president, with Secretary Daniels's concurrence, had denied the British request that Sims become an honorary member of the board of the Admiralty in November 1917.[119]

Sims enlisted the support of Walter Page, the U.S. ambassador to Great Britain, in an attempt to pressure Washington into reconsidering the appointment, but to no avail. Wilson explained to Page, "The English persist in thinking of the United States as an English people, but of course they are not and I am afraid that our people would resent and misunderstand what they would interpret as a digestion of Sims into the British official organization."[120] Sims finally dropped the matter, but he apparently never forgave Daniels for opposing the appointment.[121]

No record exists of Rodman's reaction to the department's refusal to promote him. He must have been disappointed, but he did not make any formal protest. When on convoy duty with the American squadron, the British officers in command of cruiser divisions and destroyer flotillas adopted the practice of reporting to Rodman that they waived rank and were glad to serve under him.[122]

*

The hard work of the American battleships since joining the Grand Fleet eventually began to pay off. The American ships were becoming an integral part of the British fleet, and the level of tactical cooperation they achieved had gained notice. Delegates to the Allied Naval Council paid a fine tribute to the unprecedented level of cooperation among the two navies of the Grand Fleet during a conference in April 1918.

In the wake of the peace of Brest-Litovsk, the Entente powers were concerned that the Russian Black Sea Fleet was in danger of falling into German hands, thus endangering the British Aegean squadron.[123] The simple solution would be to redistribute the naval forces in the Mediter-ranean.[124] The French were willing to send six battleships to the Italian-led Adriatic force in support of the British in the Aegean, provided they could be replaced in the western Mediterranean by four Italian battle-ships. The Italians were willing to make their battleships available, but only in an emergency. Furthermore, they were recalcitrant about having their battleships integrated into the French fleet.[125] They refused to serve under anyone other than an Italian commander in chief. The French in turn would not place their larger fleet under an Italian commander. The British attempted to resolve the impasse by suggesting Jellicoe as Med-iterranean "admiralissimo," but neither the French *nor* the Italians were interested in having a British commander in chief.[126]

The British and American delegates to the Allied Naval Council at-tempted to inspire Franco-Italian naval cooperation by pointing to the example of the American Sixth Battle Squadron. The First Sea Lord in-structed the British naval delegate to "point out to them the very great success which has accrued from the American battleships being incor-porated into the Grand Fleet, how they work, on what excellent terms are the admirals, officers, and men with each other; and how, far from any friction arising, the elements have mingled together and produced nothing but good results."[127]

The Italians never did agree to strengthen the French fleet. They were too proud to impose restrictions on their battle squadron or to place their ships under a French admiral. No fleet can be effective without unified command, and because of national pride, the French and Italians were incapable of the level of cooperation and effectiveness that the American squadron with the Grand Fleet achieved.[128]

Continuing concerns that the disposition of the Russian fleet would strengthen German naval power again raised the question of dispatching more U.S. dreadnoughts to European waters. Rodman suggested that if additional U.S. battleships were going to reinforce the Grand Fleet and Mediterranean Fleet, then the Navy Department should send them at once. He explained that new forces would require at least a couple of months to adapt to the new conditions. Rodman made it clear he was not suggesting that U.S. battleships were inferior to their British coun-terparts, but simply that assimilating new methods, especially in com-munications, would take time.[129]

Following the same logic, in early June the Plans Division of the Admiralty urged that the U.S. Navy be requested to send its remaining dreadnoughts to Europe, including all five oil-burners and three of the five coal-burners (the two others being too slow to operate with a modern fleet). The planners stressed that if events were likely to make additional U.S. battleships necessary, they should come over to Britain as soon as possible and not wait for an emergency. They noted that the experience of the Sixth Battle Squadron indicated that they needed at least four months of work before they were efficient. Among the situations that could necessitate the need for more battleships were the possibility of enemy possession of the French channel coast (the German spring offensive was still threatening Allied positions) and German acquisition of the Russian Baltic and Black Sea Fleets. To justify their argument, the planners stressed, "We cannot be too strong in the decisive area." They proposed that more U.S. battleships would make it possible to form a southern battle squadron. Furthermore, they produced figures to prove that problems of supply and shortage of destroyers were not insurmountable.

Admiral Fremantle, the deputy chief of the naval staff, pointed out to the Plans Division that Beatty had not considered the American ships as equivalent to British ships. Therefore, the addition of eight more U.S. dreadnoughts would intensify the difficulties of integration and would not compensate the Grand Fleet for the loss of a squadron to the south. Probably because of Fremantle's dissenting opinion, the Admiralty considered that the difficulties of assimilating more U.S. battleships outweighed the benefits, and took no action on the proposal of the Plans Division.[130]

The poor gunnery of the American squadron was the primary reason for the Admiralty's low opinion, but the gunnery was steadily improving. On 20 March the Sixth Battle Squadron held full-caliber firings with reduced charges and concentrated in pairs. According to Rodman, "It was a decided success, most encouraging, and shows a most gratifying improvement over last performances."[131] In the quarterly battle efficiency inspection held on 29 April, the ships showed marked improvement in battery and fire control exercises. Rodman reported that their efficiency was "not only steadily improving, but has reached such a high standard that inspires confidence in their ability to render good accounts of themselves when the time comes."[132]

During the full-caliber firing on Thursday, 27 June, the Sixth Battle Squadron performed better still. Like other practices, this one simulated war conditions, and the firing took place without knowledge of the opening range. The distance to target was 16,000 to 17,500 yards. Rodman proudly reported, "The firing was exceptionally fine, most encouraging and much better than we have ever done previously."[133] Months of determined effort to improve their gunnery was finally bearing fruit.

The American battleships were benefiting from their time in the war zone. Rodman was eager to learn from the British. He understood the value of adapting British methods and experience, learned in four years of warfare. Nothing can prepare ships and men like actual service in war conditions. In six months of service with the Grand Fleet, the U.S. battleships gained valuable experience in military operations carried out in the battleground of the North Sea. Their experience would eventually benefit the rest of the U.S. battle fleet. The service of the U.S. battleships in the war zone revealed deficiencies that might never have come to light during exercises with the Atlantic Fleet.

Integration into the Grand Fleet was a monumental task. Besides having to learn new procedures, tactics, and policies, the Americans had had to become an integral part of a foreign fleet while maintaining their own organization and traditions. During their first six months, the American dreadnoughts serving with the Grand Fleet achieved an unprecedented level of tactical cooperation. They were "learning the ropes" and had become an integral part of the British Grand Fleet.

3

EARNING RESPECT

U.S. Battleships with the Grand Fleet, July 1918
to the Surrender of the High Seas Fleet

*

During the summer and fall of 1918, the Grand Fleet remained watchful, hoping to force a decision with the High Seas Fleet. The British fleet was now a stronger force than at Jutland. British battle cruisers were still inferior to their German counterparts, but the fleet had new armor-piercing shells that promised to be capable of penetrating German armor. While the morale of the inactive High Seas Fleet was eroding, the morale of the Grand Fleet remained high. Constant gunnery drills and frequent fleet maneuvers increased the efficiency of the British and American ships with each passing day.

*

The Sixth Battle Squadron, with its destroyer screen and the Sixth Light Cruiser Squadron, sailed at 0800 on Sunday, 30 June, in support of the first American minelaying expedition in the North Sea.[1] The minelayers for the expedition were the old converted cruiser *San Francisco* and the converted liners *Canonicus, Canandaigua,* and *Housatonic.* They belonged to Mine Squadron One of the Atlantic Fleet, under the command of Capt. Reginald Belknap, based at Inverness and Cromarty.[2]

The northern barrage would eventually stretch 250 miles between the Orkney Islands and Scandinavian territorial waters. A 130-mile sector of this was completely an American operation; the remainder was a joint undertaking with the British. The Navy Department had high hopes that the North Sea barrage would greatly hamper U-boat operations, and the barrage became one of the major U.S. naval efforts of the war. By the time of the armistice, the U.S. Mine Force, under Rear Adm.

Joseph Strauss, had laid 56,611 of the 70,263 mines in the barrage. The total cost was a staggering forty million dollars, but the return on this investment was only six submarines confirmed sunk.[3]

Because the minelaying forces would necessarily have to operate within the range of German surface raiders, just as the Scandinavian convoys did, they needed a heavy covering force. The danger to the covering force protecting the minelayers would be essentially the same as to the force protecting the Scandinavian convoys. Interestingly, the Navy Department never seemed to question the need for battleships to protect the U.S. Mine Force, the way they did the use of a battleship escort for the Scandinavian convoys. Perhaps they had less concern about a raid against the minelaying force because its operations were more sporadic than the convoy sailings.

After making contact with the mining force in the early afternoon of June 30, the battleships took station twenty miles southeast of the minelayers, between the force and German waters. Because the minelaying force could steam at only 13 knots, the battleships zigzagged at 17 knots to keep position. The light cruisers took station to the southeast of the battleships.

At 1625, as the squadron steamed in line abreast, the *Wyoming* and the U.S. destroyer *Parker* sighted a periscope. The *Delaware*, *Florida*, and *Wyoming* opened fire at a range of 1,400 yards and the destroyers dropped six depth charges. The squadron maneuvered to avoid a possible torpedo attack and then continued on course.

An hour later, the *Florida* reported another submarine sighting and opened fire. The *Delaware* and *Texas* opened fire in the same direction, although they did not sight anything. This time the destroyers dropped ten depth charges, again without apparent results.[4]

Admiral Rodman believed that both sightings were false alarms. He noted that before each sighting, the squadron had just made a turn, and in conjunction with the wind direction, the disturbance in the water could have resembled a submarine wake. The battleships may have been firing at their own wakes rather than the wake of a U-boat. After returning to port and interviewing the high-ranking officers involved, however, Rodman changed his mind and decided that the submarine sightings were genuine. The officers who sighted the U-boat insisted that they saw it distinctly, and the commander of the destroyer leader also believed he saw a submarine before making his depth-charge attack. The Admiralty also reported having located an enemy submarine in the same vicinity.[5]

Reviewing German records, this sighting could have been the U-70, which was passing through the eastern side of the American sector of the northern barrage at the time, but U-70 did not report any warships that day. Therefore, this particular sighting probably was a false alarm.[6]

Upon reaching the Scandinavian coast in the early morning hours of the next day, the minelayers began sowing their mines and the covering force maintained its position to the south. In just two-and-a-half hours they laid a double line of 2,200 mines. Between 0900 and 0930, the battleships and their screen sighted as many as five floating mines. Captain Wiley of the *Wyoming* recalled that he feared mines more than any other threat in the North Sea. Both sides sowed an enormous number of mines during the war, many of which broke free of their moorings because of the rough seas.[7]

The covering force did double duty on the return voyage. They linked up with the westbound Scandinavian convoy "HZ40" on the afternoon of July 1, and supported it until 2200. The Sixth Battle Squadron arrived at Scapa Flow on 2 July at 0300.[8]

*

The officers and men of the Sixth Battle Squadron enjoyed a couple of days' respite from all drills and exercises to celebrate the Fourth of July. The squadron transferred its anchorage to the north shore of Scapa Flow to be as near as possible to Kirkwall, the principal town. Four hours of liberty were granted to two hundred men from each ship twice a day. The main attraction was the Temperance Hotel, the only place in town where a drink could be had.[9] Rodman reported that both officers and men appreciated having a holiday after a strenuous seven months in the war zone. He was also pleased to report that the conduct of the men while in Kirkwall was excellent. Some of the local dignitaries reported to him that they had never seen such exemplary conduct.

Admiral Beatty sent a cordial message of greetings on "this greatest of Liberty Days" to Rodman and the Sixth Battle Squadron. In addition, a representative body of flag officers from the Grand Fleet paid an official visit to the *New York*. In response to the expressions of British goodwill, Rodman reported, "It is gratifying to state that no more cordial relations could exist than those which obtain between the American and British divisions of this Force."[10]

The men of the American squadron also enjoyed ten days of leave when their individual ships rotated to Newcastle for a refit. The *Delaware*, for example, docked at Newcastle in April. Overall, the *Delaware*'s crew made a good impression on the locals. The commanding officer reported only one infraction "due to overtime or rum," and stated that he received many compliments from the shore authorities on the fine behavior of the men.[11] Some of the men availed themselves of the wrong attractions, however. Rodman reported that all of the ships experienced an unusually high number of venereal disease cases after visiting Newcastle. He suggested that the Navy do a better job of warning the men against the dangers of seaports.[12]

One of the reasons for the high morale of the Grand Fleet, as opposed to that of the High Seas Fleet, was that the officers took an interest in providing amusements for the men to relieve the tedium of remaining at base on alert. Sporting events were the principal entertainment, with some events including the entire fleet in competition. The fleet track meet was a big event, and the Sixth Battle Squadron took second place.

The big event of the year was the Grand Fleet boxing championship, held at Rosyth dockyard on 28 and 29 July. There was seating available for only seven thousand spectators, so signal flags sent the results to the ships. The Sixth Battle Squadron gave a fine account of itself. An engineman from the *Florida* won the lightweight title, a chief carpenter's mate from the *New York* won the middleweight title, and a fireman, also from the *New York*, reached the heavyweight finals.[13]

Besides sporting events, all of the ships in the squadron produced amateur theatricals, including vaudeville acts and minstrel shows. In addition, motion picture shows were available on almost a daily basis. When at Rosyth and not on short notice, officers could avail themselves of liberty whenever it did not interfere with their duties and the men had an afternoon of liberty once every sixteen days. The vicinity of Rosyth offered small dances, music performances, tennis, and excellent golf links.[14]

The Sixth Battle Squadron imported some American sports for its recreation at Rosyth. The British allotted the American squadron sports fields, which soon became a football field and baseball diamond. The squadron had a baseball league that played seventeen games during the summer. The *Texas* won the squadron championship, but lost to the visiting team from naval headquarters in London. Organized football games began in the fall. Some of the Americans attempted European football (soccer) with the British, although there is no record of their performance in the game.[15]

The Grand Fleet received two royal visits in July. The fleet had again moved from Scapa Flow to Rosyth, carrying out maneuvers and fire-concentration exercises during the journey south. On Monday, 8 July, the king and queen of Belgium reviewed the fleet from a destroyer. The next day the sovereigns inspected several ships in the fleet, including the *New York.* The king and queen spent an hour touring the American flagship and received an appropriate welcome from their hosts.[16]

Two weeks later, King George V visited his fleet, his fourth visit to the fleet since hostilities began. The king embarked in the destroyer *Oak* on Monday, 22 July, and inspected the fleet. As he passed, each ship's band played "God Save the King," while the crews gave three cheers for His Majesty. At 1215 there was an investiture ceremony on board Beatty's flagship, *Queen Elizabeth.* When His Majesty came on deck, the honor guard presented arms, the band played the national anthem, and all officers saluted the sovereign. The king presented decorations from a platform erected aft of the assembled host. The first recipient was Admiral Rodman. The king invested him as a knight commander of the Order of the Bath, the highest decoration awarded that day.[17]

After having lunch aboard *Queen Elizabeth,* the king visited the *New York* for an hour. He inspected her engine and fire-rooms and was impressed, remarking to Rodman, "Admiral, your fire-room is as clean as a dining room." As a former officer in the Royal Navy, the king was well qualified to make such a judgment. Upon Rodman's request, the king condescended to shovel coal into the furnace, as he had done as the Duke of York on one of the battle cruisers. Amid the cheers of the stokers, the king of England graciously shoveled coal into the furnace of an American battleship. After the official inspection, the king and his party adjourned to Rodman's cabin for coffee, a smoke, and some yarn-swapping. Rodman recalled in his memoir that the king seemed to especially enjoy this session of casual conversation.[18]

Following his departure, the king sent a message of encouragement to the officers and men of the Grand Fleet. He began his message with reference to the American squadron: "I am happy to have found myself once more with the Grand Fleet, and this pleasure has been increased by the opportunity I have had of seeing the splendid ships of the United States in line with our own, and of meeting Admiral Rodman together with the officers and men under him. We value their comradeship and are proud of their achievements." Beatty thanked the king for his message and replied, "We are glad that Your Majesty should have been able personally to observe our complete accord with the United States Squadron and the firm friendship which binds their officers and men to Your own."[19]

These expressions reflected, and reinforced, the goodwill that truly did exist between the Americans and British serving in the Grand Fleet. An amusing example of the rapport between Beatty and Rodman involved British and American labor delegations that visited the Grand Fleet. On a tour of the *New York*, a British labor leader was making a short speech in Rodman's cabin. He spoke of the folly of the German kaiser, and then to emphasize his point, turned and spat upon the admiral's carpet! Not long afterwards, American labor leaders, led by the famous head of the American Federation of Labor, Samuel Gompers, dined aboard the *Queen Elizabeth* with Admiral Beatty. When after-dinner cigars were passed, Gompers smelled his, pinched it, and proclaimed it an inferior cigar: "I know a good cigar when I see one. You know, Admiral, I know whereof I speak because I am a cigar-maker by trade." During the next meeting between Beatty and Rodman, Beatty said, "You know, Rodman, I think that you and I are about even. Our labor leader spat on your rug, and your labor leader, a guest at my table, was ill-mannered enough to criticize my cigar." Declaring that they were indeed even, the two admirals shook hands on it.[20]

✻

On 29 July a new member joined the Sixth Battle Squadron. The *Arkansas*, under the command of Capt. W. H. G. Bullard, arrived from the United States to relieve the *Delaware*. The *Arkansas*, sister ship of the *Wyoming*, gave better balance to the fleet in terms of paired calibers for fire concentration. The *Delaware* and *Florida* (12-inch/45 caliber) had constituted a matched pair, with the *Wyoming* (12-inch/50 caliber) as a spare. Now the two *Wyoming*-class ships were a pair, with the *Florida* as a spare.

The *Arkansas* had sailed from Hampton Roads on 14 July with fourteen important passengers, members of the House naval committee.[21] During their passage from Scapa Flow to Rosyth, the congressmen had an exciting introduction to the war zone. At around 2100 on 28 July, the officer of the deck sounded the submarine alarm. The *Arkansas* immediately opened fire on an object on the port quarter. Upon reaching the navigation bridge, Captain Bullard ordered "emergency full-ahead" and the ship soon made 21 knots. While turning away from the direction of the sighting, the captain himself saw the wake of a slowly submerging submarine. At the same time, a lookout reported a torpedo running directly toward the ship. The *Arkansas* turned to port, and the lookout reported the torpedo running to starboard and clear of the ship.

Bullard later interrogated the lookouts and gun crews. The gun crews reported distinctly seeing a periscope, and three witnesses verified the torpedo sighting. The escorting British destroyers, however, assumed the incident was just another U-boat scare typical of newcomers to the war zone. In his report to Rodman, Bullard complained of the lack of seriousness on the part of their escort.[22] The British escorts perhaps should have assumed that the sighting was genuine, but there was in fact no U-boat attack. None of the U-boats operating in the area that day reported sighting any warships.[23]

The *Arkansas* safely joined the American squadron at noon on the twenty-ninth of July. The next day the *Delaware*, with the British destroyers *Rowena* and *Restless*, left the Grand Fleet and began her return voyage to the United States. The *Delaware* parted company with her escort on 1 August and arrived at Hampton Roads on 12 August.[24]

On Thursday, 8 August, the Fifth and Sixth Battle Squadrons together acted as escort for a joint British and American minelaying operation in the northern barrage. The covering force was under the command of Vice Adm. Hugh Evan-Thomas, commander of the Fifth Squadron. The British First Minelaying Squadron and seven destroyers, and the U.S. Minelaying Squadron Two and its screen of twelve destroyers, simultaneously left their respective bases in the early morning.

The two minelaying squadrons had separate minefields to lay. The battleships took station near the British minelayers and the Second Light Cruiser Squadron and five destroyers from Scapa Flow provided direct support for the American minelayers.[25]

On the first night of the mission, the battleships were in line-ahead and steaming at 16.5 knots. At 2212 in the low twilight, the navigator of the *Florida* sighted the wake of a torpedo. He was positive it was a torpedo because the discharged bubbles were distinctly visible in the wake. The torpedo traveled from the port side and passed either ahead of or just under the ship. A lookout spotted a periscope on the port side nearly at the same time. Both the *New York* and *Florida* reported the attack to their escorts, which investigated but did not sight anything, nor did they drop any depth charges. The remainder of the operation was without incident.[26]

After returning to Rosyth, the commander of the Fifth Battle Squadron, Evan-Thomas, investigated the incident. He inquired of the commander of the XV Flotilla about the actions of the destroyer screen.[27] The flotilla commander examined the officers commanding the two destroyers in the vicinity of the incident, *Undine* and *Ulysses*, and asked why they had not dropped depth charges. Both officers justified their actions, or lack of action, by explaining that the squadron had already passed out of danger before they began their search. Also, they suspected any submarine would have been on the surface because they considered it too dark to use periscopes. Consequently, they reasoned, depth charges would have forced the U-boat to submerge, making it more difficult to locate.[28]

The flotilla commander did not accept their explanations. He reported to Evans-Thomas, "I regret I do not concur in the action of either of these officers in not dropping depth charges." He stated that although the battleships may have passed out of danger before they received a signal, the destroyers should have dropped four depth charges each on the estimated position of the sighting.[29] After the matter came to Beatty's attention, he instructed Evans-Thomas to "inform the commanding officers of *Undine* and *Ulysses* that depth charges should have been dropped on the occasion of the submarine attack on Sixth Battle Squadron."[30] This rebuke from the commander in chief must have encouraged the destroyer captains to take submarine sightings with more gravity.

One suspects that the newcomers to the war had cried wolf too many times, and now their escorts did not take them seriously enough. Whether this was justifiable or not, it would appear that once again there was no wolf. No U-boats in the vicinity reported sighting warships that day.[31]

*

Throughout the summer, the Sixth Battle Squadron carried out gunnery exercises on a weekly basis. These practices consisted of sub-caliber concentration, spotting, and rangefinding exercises. Mock destroyer and submarine attacks during sub-caliber firings added realism to the practices. Further, the advent of air power was already adding another dimension to naval tactics. On several occasions, aircraft simulated attacks on the bridges and other exposed positions of the ships. The principal role of aircraft at this time was still spotting and reconnaissance, but naval leaders already recognized the potential for an offensive role against surface ships. U.S. battleships had 3-inch antiaircraft guns mounted after 1916. While with the Grand Fleet, the ships received portable machine guns for additional protection against air attack.[32]

For long-range spotting, the ships in the Grand Fleet relied upon towed kite balloons. Balloons were installed on ships in the Sixth Battle Squadron in the late spring and U.S. officers attended balloon training at Roehampton.[33] The observation balloons greatly facilitated accurate spotting, but Rodman reported a number of limitations on their use. One exercise revealed that an observation balloon could be a handicap as well as an advantage. The exercise involved two forces: a firing squadron, and an attacking "enemy" force of one battleship and two destroyer divisions. When the attacking force laid a heavy smoke screen that obscured it from the firing squadron, the balloon gave away the location of the firing squadron to the "enemy," but could not see the attacking force through the smoke. Rodman also recognized that observation balloons would be vulnerable to hostile aircraft because they lacked freedom of movement.[34] Another problem with the hydrogen-filled balloons was their flammability. On 9 July, just before the visit of the king and queen of Belgium, lightning struck the *New York*'s kite balloon and sent it plunging in flames into the water from a height of about 1,200 feet. Lightning also destroyed the *Barham*'s balloon that same day.[35]

Despite these limitations, kite balloons remained the principal means of spotting. Aircraft, the main alternative, had serious limitations of their own. Several ships in the Grand Fleet, including the *Texas*, were fitted with flying-off platforms on turret roofs, but these fighters were intended to destroy German reconnaissance seaplanes and zeppelins, not to provide reconnaissance and spotting. Launching was possible but *retrieval* was not. The pilots had to ditch their planes after the flight, unless within range of a land base. This necessarily restricted the shipborne aircraft to emergency, one-time use. HMS *Argus*, the first carrier that could reliably launch and recover its planes, was not commissioned until September 1918, and carrier operations were still in their infancy when the war ended.[36]

The Sixth Battle Squadron engaged in several operations in the North Sea between August and the armistice. The Grand Fleet carried out maneuvers in the North Sea on 22–23 August, and again on 24 September. During the September exercise, the Red Fleet from Rosyth, including the Sixth Battle Squadron, engaged the Blue Fleet from Scapa Flow, consisting of the Fourth Battle Squadron and Second Battle Cruiser Squadron and representing the High Seas Fleet. An interesting aspect of this operation was the use of aircraft. At 0950, aircraft from the carrier *Furious* reported the "enemy" Blue Fleet. The Red Fleet did not alter course, however, until light cruisers had confirmed the location of the Blue Fleet ten minutes later, because the air reconnaissance was not considered completely reliable. At 1020, the opposing battle cruiser forces engaged each other at a range of 23,000 yards, closing to 15,000 yards, followed by torpedo attacks. At noon the main fleets spotted each other out of the mist at 21,000 yards and engaged each other down to a range of 14,000 yards, whereupon destroyers and cruisers in the van attacked the blue battle line.[37]

In his remarks on the exercise, Beatty observed that the distribution of fire was better than in earlier maneuvers, but some individual ships in the center of the red battle line still made "serious mistakes" by concentrating their fire on the wrong target. The exercise shows the great reliance that the British placed on rapidly concentrating the most fire possible to inflict maximum damage to any visible portion of the enemy fleet. The fire-concentration rules of the Grand Fleet were designed to bring about a decisive action while favorable conditions existed and before smoke could obscure the view of the enemy or communications had a chance to break down. At the next Jutland, Beatty did not want poor visibility and confusion to rob him of victory.[38]

After receiving a report that three large enemy vessels were loose on the North Sea on Saturday evening, 12 October, the Sixth Battle Squadron, Second Battle Cruiser Squadron, and Third Light Cruiser Squadron sortied from Scapa Flow "with the hopes of intercepting and engaging the enemy." The ships scouted the passage between the Orkneys and Shetlands all night.[39] Storm warnings were already flying when they left and the weather continued to worsen. By noon the next day, the weather was so rough that the force had to reduce speed to 12 knots for the safety of the destroyers. The force never sighted any raiders, and finally set a course back to Scapa Flow.[40] The report that German raiders had escaped into the North Sea was false.[41]

As *New York* led the squadron back into Pentland Firth at 1742 on 14 October, she experienced a terrific underwater blow on the starboard quarter, followed by another to the stern. The latter broke off two propeller blades, forcing *New York* to run on one engine at no more than 12 knots. It was immediately clear that the ship had struck a submerged object, but the squadron was steaming in mid-channel in 33 fathoms of water, which precluded the possibility of striking a wreck. Therefore, the *New York* must have collided with a submerged U-boat.

Rodman's report on the incident explains how such a collision could have happened. First of all, the strong current in Pentland Firth made handling a U-boat very difficult. Vertical movement was especially dangerous, so submarines would not submerge to a great depth while in Pentland Firth. As it was getting dark, it is likely the U-boat had surfaced to take bearings, knowing there was little chance of being detected in the failing light. At the time, the battleships were in the process of steering southwest around Old Head and approaching Hoxa Sound, the entrance to Scapa Flow. The speed of the squadron at the time was 18 knots, double the speed of a submarine. A U-boat standing to the westward at that locality would not have seen the approaching battleships until they were well on to her. The sudden appearance of warships would have compelled the U-boat to submerge, but it would probably have maintained its former course because of the danger in maneuvering underwater in the strong current. Just before the collision, the *New York* had changed to a northwestward course, which probably crossed the track of the submarine. Rodman reported that, in his opinion and Beatty's opinion as well, the submarine had rammed its bow into the *New York*'s side, then drifted aft and been struck with the propeller. The collision must have inflicted such damage to the U-boat that she became unmanageable and sank.[42]

The Germans used UB-class coastal submarines for operations along the Scottish coast, including Pentland Firth and the Firth of Forth. During the middle of October, they lost two coastal submarines, UB-113 and UB-123, to unknown causes. One of these was probably the submarine that collided with the *New York*.[43]

The next day, Tuesday the fifteenth, Rodman transferred his flag to the *Wyoming*, and the *New York* departed for Rosyth and repairs. The *New York*, still running on one engine and with additional escort owing to her reduced speed, left Scapa Flow at 1300. At 0100, a U-boat fired three torpedoes at the wounded ship, all of which passed ahead of her. Normally, the ship would have been cruising at 16 knots rather than 12, and the U-boat commander probably misjudged the battleship's speed. The captain and gunnery officer, among others, clearly saw the torpedo wakes in the bright moonlight. A patrol spotted a submarine in the vicinity at about the same time as the attack.[44] When the *New York* went into dry dock at Rosyth later on Wednesday morning, a large dent was found in the bottom of the hull, corresponding with the damage that the bow of a submarine would make. The *New York* was fortunate to have such minor damage after two close calls.[45]

During the *New York*'s absence, the remainder of the squadron carried out their scheduled full-caliber practice in Pentland Firth. The firing was at 11,000 yards with reduced charges and concentrated in pairs. Each ship was allotted eight salvos. The *Texas*'s shooting was excellent and the *Wyoming*'s was almost as good. The *Arkansas*, however, made a poor showing at her first full-caliber shoot. She suffered from all of the deficiencies that had plagued the American squadron when it first arrived in the war zone. The poor handling of the *Arkansas* interfered with the *Florida*'s shooting as well.

The *Arkansas* suffered from a communication breakdown between the conning tower and engine room. The number of revolutions the captain ordered was confused with the base course during transmission to the engine room, which resulted in the ship slowing suddenly and blanketing the *Florida*'s fire. The plotting room should have detected the discrepancy between real and assumed speed, but did not. Rodman reported to the Navy Department: "I can see no possible excuse for such a discrepancy in the initial range except sheer carelessness or inefficiency."[46] Moreover, there was every opportunity for rangefinder corrections, but the spotters also failed. Apparently, one of the spotters had poor eyesight. Rodman could not understand how a man with such poor vision could have become the *Arkansas*'s spotter. The *Arkansas* was clearly not at a high state of battle efficiency. Neither did the *Florida* completely escape criticism. Rodman determined that the *Florida* should have been able to cope with a sharp decrease of speed without warning, because such an emergency would possibly happen in battle.

Nevertheless, the practice was not a failure. Not only did the *Texas* and *Wyoming* perform well, the average pattern of shot for the whole squadron was down to 600 yards, a significant reduction from earlier practices, although still not as good as the British average.[47] The *New York* and the *Arkansas* completed a full-caliber practice on 7 November, the last time the American battleships fired their main batteries while with the Grand Fleet. The *New York*'s shooting was very good, but the *Arkansas*'s shooting still "left much to be desired."[48]

As the Great War neared its end, one of the war's effects killed additional millions. The influenza epidemic of the fall and winter of 1918 was a worldwide outbreak that did not spare the Grand Fleet. The fleet averaged seven deaths per day due to influenza. The epidemic was so severe in two British battle cruisers, however, that they were practically out of commission. There were so few able-bodied men aboard them that fleet tugs had to make steam for them to supply essential services for the ships. Lt. John McCrea, aboard the *New York*, believed that had the German fleet come out to do battle during the epidemic, many ships of the Grand Fleet would not have been able to give an account of themselves.[49] Strict quarantine measures successfully limited the scope of the epidemic, however.

The ships of the American squadron were not immune to the outbreak. In early November, all but the *Florida* were in quarantine. The epidemic was especially acute aboard the *Arkansas*. The disease had spread to the *Arkansas* in late October when a draft of men from the transport *Leviathan,* a badly infected ship, temporarily quartered on her while awaiting passage on another vessel. By 9 November, the *Arkansas* had 259 influenza cases and 11 deaths. Conditions were considerably better on the other American ships. The *New York,* for example, had forty-eight cases and just one death as of 9 November.[50]

✳

While the naval war continued much as it had all year—with the Grand Fleet standing guard over the German High Seas Fleet and the convoys proceeding relentlessly across the Atlantic—events on the Western Front rapidly came to a decision toward the end of 1918. Allied troops had stopped the last German offensive in late summer. The infusion of American blood helped the Allies. The Meuse-Argonne offensive in late September made steady progress. As German resistance began to crumble, Bulgaria concluded an armistice. On 3 October Prince Max von Baden became chancellor of Germany and asked President Wilson to arrange an armistice. Wilson demanded that German armies evacuate occupied territory and that submarine attacks on passenger vessels end before he would consider any armistice. On 20 October Prince Max agreed to end unrestricted submarine warfare.[51]

Germany's naval leaders, however, did not feel the need for an armistice; they remained undefeated. They were determined that the war must not end before their final "naval Armageddon" with the Grand Fleet. When the end of the submarine campaign released the U-boats for service with the fleet, Admiral Scheer, chief of the German Admiralty, considered the time ripe for the High Seas Fleet to do battle with the British fleet. On 21 October the German Admiralty informed Adm. Franz von Hipper, chief of the High Seas Fleet, that he should prepare to sortie against the Grand Fleet. Hipper determined that "an honorable fleet engagement, even if it should become a death struggle" was preferable to an inglorious end to the German fleet. Scheer did not bother to inform the kaiser or the chancellor of his momentous decision.[52]

On 24 October, German naval leaders formally adopted Hipper's plans for the last sortie, contained in "Operations Plan 19." The plan called for one destroyer group to attack the Flanders coast while another attacked the Thames estuary at daybreak on the second day of the operation. Elements of the fleet would support both attacks. The destroyer attacks would bait the Grand Fleet into the North Sea—into an ambush of twenty-five U-boats in six lines. The retiring German fleet would then draw the Grand Fleet toward Terschelling, a Dutch island in the North Sea, where the great battle would occur under conditions of German choosing.

In the end, it would not be Allied shells that defeated the German fleet, but the corrosive effects of the blockade. The long months of inactivity had undermined the morale of the High Seas Fleet to the extent that the crews of the capital ships were unreliable. When news of a "suicide sortie" leaked out to the German crewmen, a mutiny broke out that effectively removed the High Seas Fleet as a fighting force. The German sailors simply were not willing to die for nothing more than the honor of the Imperial German Navy.[53]

The mutiny forced Hipper to cancel Operation 19, and he dispersed the fleet to the Elbe, Kiel, and Wilhelmshaven. Instead of isolating the disloyal elements, however, this only served to spread the infection to the port cities. Rebellious sailors with red flags gained control of such important cities as Hanover, Hamburg, and Bremen by 7 November. On 9 November Scheer told the kaiser he could no longer rely on the navy. The kaiser bitterly replied, "I no longer have a Navy." Later that day, the last Hohenzollern ruler boarded his imperial train for exile in the Netherlands. His navy had become a double-edged sword. The kaiser had supported the navy to the point of war with Britain, but in defeat, that navy turned against its patron.[54]

By this point, even a victory against the Grand Fleet would not have altered the course of the war. The Grand Fleet would certainly have suffered losses, but just as certainly would have remained an effective and probably a superior battle fleet. Few expected that a final battle would change the ultimate course of events.

*

The debate in the Allied Naval Council over the naval terms of the armistice reopened old antagonisms between U.S. and British naval leaders. Sir Rosslyn Wemyss, the First Sea Lord, supported Beatty's proposal that the Germans surrender most of their surface fleet to the Allies. Since U.S. naval leaders feared that the British would acquire most of the surrendered ships, they supported the internment of German ships in neutral ports, rather than their surrender, until the peace conference decided their ultimate fate.

With the support of Prime Minister Lloyd George and Marshal Ferdinand Foch, internment gained favor in the Supreme War Council and became the basis of the naval terms of the armistice. Although the Allied Naval Council maintained its view that Germany should surrender its ships, political leaders recognized the wisdom of internment. The terms, which were stiff, stipulated that the flower of the High Seas Fleet—ten German dreadnoughts, all its battle cruisers, eight light cruisers, and fifty of the most modern destroyers—would be interned at a designated port, and all submarines would be surrendered. Representatives of the German government signed the armistice on 11 November 1918.[55]

Joubert McCrea, a member of one of the *Florida*'s 5-inch gun crews, wrote his parents to describe the joyful celebration after word of the armistice reached the fleet:

> Last night, thousands of whistles and sirens began roaring to the world the news of the surrender. . . . Mixed with the noise of the sirens were signal guns going off. They shot red, green, and white stars into the sky and each one would burst into many smaller stars and float lazily to the water. . . . After a while the searchlights on all the ships, hundreds of ships, and thousands of powerful searchlights began sweeping the skies. Underneath the sets of eight, ten, or twelve lights, you could make out the bulky form of a battle wagon alive with men singing and shouting themselves hoarse.[56]

Because no neutral nation would accept the mutinous German fleet, the Allies chose Scapa Flow as the location of the fleet's internment. On 15 and 16 November, Beatty met Hipper's representative, Rear Adm. Hugo Meurer, to arrange for the surrender of Germany's ships. Beatty was courteous during the negotiations, but all business. The German admiral looked as if he were ill. The Germans agreed to surrender to Beatty in the Firth of Forth, prior to their transfer to Scapa Flow for internment until the peace conference decided their fate.[57]

*

On Wednesday, 20 November, the king and queen of England and the Prince of Wales joined the Grand Fleet during their hour of triumph. After reviewing the fleet from the destroyer *Oak*, the royal family had lunch aboard the *Queen Elizabeth*. In the afternoon, the king and prince visited the *New York* for a half-hour.[58] Admiral Sims and members of his staff also visited the Sixth Battle Squadron. Sims remained aboard the *New York* to witness the big event on the next day: "Operation ZZ"—the surrender of the German High Seas Fleet.[59]

At 0830 the Grand Fleet arrived at the appointed rendezvous 40 miles east of May Island. The fleet formed two great parallel columns, 6 miles apart. The vast armada, which included the forces from Harwich, Dover, and the Channel, included 370 ships and 90,000 men. Marder states that "such a force had never been collected before." The ships hoisted every battle flag they had. It must have been an inspiring sight. The American battleships occupied the center of the northern line, between the Fifth and the Second battle squadrons.[60]

At 0930 the British light cruiser *Cardiff* met the once-proud German battle fleet and led them between the two victorious columns. The ships of the Grand Fleet remained at battle stations with the great guns empty, but with powder and shell resting in the loading trays, ready to be rammed home. The Germans were to have removed their breech blocks and fire control equipment, and to have discharged all ammunition. Nevertheless, Admiral Beatty did not trust them. Who could believe the Imperial German Navy would meekly surrender without a battle? In Rodman's words: "It was hard to realize that the ships which we had expected and hoped to engage, would all be given up without a struggle or fleet action, and surrender without a fight." But there was no last act of defiance. The vast funeral procession turned and proceeded into the Firth of Forth. Beatty then made the signal to the Germans: "The German flag will be hauled down at sunset today, Thursday, and will not be hoisted again without permission."[61]

When the German ensigns came down at sunset, all hands aboard *Queen Elizabeth* cheered the commander in chief. Beatty smiled and said, "I always told you they would have to come out."[62] At a thanksgiving service that evening, Beatty issued a message of congratulations to the officers and men of the Grand Fleet:

> The greatness of this achievement is in no way lessened by the fact that the final episode did not take the form of a fleet action. Although deprived of this

opportunity, which we had so long and eagerly awaited, and of striking the final blow for the freedom of the world, we may derive satisfaction from the
singular tribute which the enemy has accorded to the Grand Fleet. His surrender without joining us in action is a testimony to the prestige and efficiency of the fleet without parallel in history, and it is to be remembered that
this testimony has been accorded by those who were in the best position to
judge.[63]

One would think the ignominious surrender of the High Seas Fleet
would have caused nothing but jubilation in the Grand Fleet, but the
feelings were mixed. On the occasion of the armistice, Beatty declared,
"The Fleet, my Fleet, is brokenhearted." After witnessing the surrender
of the German fleet, Joubert McCrea wrote in his diary: "I never hoped
to meet them this way, I wanted to fight them."[64]

Wemyss explained in his memoir why there was no joy in the victory:
"They had looked for a Trafalgar—for a defeat of the German Fleet in
which they would have played a prominent and proud part. What they
got was a victory far more crushing than any Trafalgar and with none of
its attendant losses on our part—but also without any of the personal
glory which would have been attached to the survivors."[65] The fact remains that the Grand Fleet, the American squadron among them,
achieved an unparalleled naval victory. Victory without glory, after all, is
victory nonetheless.

✳

Coming soon after the dramatic surrender of the German fleet, and with
the Americans making preparations to leave the Grand Fleet, Thanksgiving was a special occasion. Beatty decided that every ship in the Grand
Fleet would host officers and men of the American ships for Thanksgiving dinner. Bernhard Bieri, a young officer aboard the *Texas*, remembered the good time had by all. As the time came for the Americans to
board their boats to return to their ship, the British insisted that they
were broken down, and that efforts to get them running were unsuccessful. The party continued until the early morning hours before the alleged malfunctioning boats were running again.[66]

On 1 December 1918, it was time for the American squadron to leave
the Grand Fleet. The commander in chief came aboard *New York* to

thank the officers and men of the Sixth Battle Squadron for their service and to give them a heartfelt farewell:

> I know quite well that you, as well as all of your comrades, were bitterly disappointed at not being able to give effect to that efficiency that you have so well maintained. It was a most disappointing day. It was a pitiful day to see those great ships coming in like sheep being herded by dogs to their fold, without an effort on anybody's part; but it was a day that everybody could be proud of. . . . I had always certain misgivings [that the German fleet would never submit to battle], and when the Sixth Battle Squadron became part of the Grand Fleet those misgivings were doubly strengthened, and I knew then they would throw up their hands. Apparently, the Sixth Battle Squadron was the straw that broke the camel's back. . . . You will return to your own shores; and I hope in the sunshine, which Admiral Rodman tells me always shines there, you won't forget your comrades of the mist and your pleasant associations of the North Sea.[67]

Rodman wrote a farewell to Beatty expressing his appreciation and esteem:

> Your constant thoughtfulness and your numberless courtesies have made our path clear, and I deeply appreciate your valuable assistance in all matters affecting the amalgamation of this force into the Grand Fleet from the very first day of our arrival. We leave with the pleasantest memories of a happy and instructive year under your able guidance and I go with the feeling that I am parting from tried and true friends in you, and my other brother officers of the Grand Fleet.[68]

As the U.S. battleships steamed out from Rosyth for the last time, the British and American ships exchanged last-minute farewells. On behalf of the officers and men in the British fleet, Beatty signaled: "Your comrades in the Grand Fleet regret your departure. We trust it is only temporary and that the interchange of squadrons from the two great fleets of the Anglo Saxon Race may be repeated."[69] Rodman answered with a signal on behalf of the Sixth Battle Squadron: "We will never forget the hospitality which has made us feel as a part of one big family and we intend to maintain that relation for all time."[70]

Remarkable harmony existed between the Americans and their comrades in the Grand Fleet. The above testimonials of mutual regard were apparently quite sincere. As Rodman expressed it, "As time wore on, our friendship ripened into a fellowship and comradeship, which, in turn, became a brotherhood."[71] The two admirals, Beatty and Rodman, not only worked well together, they became friends. This spirit of comradeship became the dominant feature of the amalgamation of the U.S. battleships into the Grand Fleet, and it explains why their operational cooperation was such an unprecedented success. Rodman deserves much credit for the harmony because of his efforts to prevent any rivalries, misunderstandings, or jealousy. His willingness to take orders from the British commander in chief and benefit from British war experience greatly facilitated the integration of the U.S. battleships into the Grand Fleet. Had Rodman been a contentious or proud person, the American squadron would never have become so fully integrated into the Grand Fleet.

Beatty also deserves credit for the successful cooperation of the American battleships with the British fleet. Beatty was a very capable leader of men who understood the importance of morale. He was willing to make the American squadron an integral part of Grand Fleet operations even while he had concerns about its efficiency. He was careful to keep his criticisms private but quick to lend encouragement and praise. In remarking upon the service of the American squadron with the Grand Fleet, Alfred Lord Chatfield remarked, "Nothing would have been easier than a clash of ideas, of principles of fighting, of routine methods between two Services which had never been at sea together and had been trained in completely different environments."[72] Because both Beatty and Rodman worked to ensure that no clash occurred, harmony was the dominant note in the operational cooperation of the American squadron with the Grand Fleet.

Vice Adm. John McCrea, looking back on a lifetime of service in the U.S. Navy, remembered his time with Grand Fleet as a junior officer as a fond memory and valuable experience:

> Service in the Grand Fleet was professionally beneficial to all of us, and at the same time, many of the friendships were made at that time which have persisted throughout the years. With the passing of the years, I have often reflected on the effect service in the Grand Fleet made on all of us young officers. It was a great privilege to serve in that fine organization.[73]

The vigilance of the Grand Fleet finally paid off, but in a way that few had foreseen. A decisive fleet engagement along classical lines did not happen, but the dramatic surrender of the German fleet represented a victory that was greater than Trafalgar, and U.S. battleships had a share in that victory. The officers and men of the American squadron achieved more than just operational cooperation with the Grand Fleet, they took their place in the British battle line as comrades.

More than just an example of the splendid cooperation of two allies, the amalgamation of the American squadron into the Grand Fleet provided officers and men with wartime experience in the finest fleet that had yet existed. Perhaps more importantly, the experience prepared future leaders in the U.S. Navy, many of whom would help lead the service to victory in the next war.

Secretary of the Navy Josephus Daniels and Chief of Naval Operations William Shepherd Benson. Daniels and Benson were initially reluctant to send a U.S. battleship division to European waters because they feared unrestricted submarine warfare would force the British to accept a separate peace and the United States would have to fight Germany alone.

Vice Adm. William Sowden Sims was the senior liaison with the British Admiralty and commander in chief of U.S. Navy forces in European waters. Sims, a notorious Anglophile, grew impatient with the Navy Department for failing to concentrate forces in European waters to support British naval strategy.

Rear Adm. Hugh Rodman commanded the American squadron with the British Grand Fleet. Rodman was a Kentuckian known for his storytelling and his seamanship. He deserves much of the credit for the smooth relations and remarkable tactical cooperation between his squadron and the British battle fleet.

Rodman with the captains of his squadron. To the left of Rodman is Capt. Archibald Scales, commander of the *Delaware*, and Capt. Henry A. Wiley, commander of the *Wyoming* and future commander in chief of the Atlantic Fleet. To the right of Rodman is Capt. Thomas Washington, commander of the *Florida*, and Capt. Charles F. Hughes, commander of Rodman's flagship the *New York* and a future chief of naval operations.

The *New York* (BB-34), *Wyoming* (BB-32), *Florida* (BB-30), and *Delaware* (BB-28) joining the British Grand Fleet at Scapa Flow on 7 December 1917 as the officers and crew of the British flagship *Queen Elizabeth* cheer their arrival.

British and American signalmen working together on the American Battleship *New York*. To operate with the Grand Fleet the Americans had to master British signals and code. *Imperial War Museum*

The American battleships attached to the Grand Fleet, steaming in line-ahead entering Rosyth, Scotland. *Imperial War Museum*

U.S. battleships during target practice. Unlike the American system at this time, the British system of target practice closely simulated battle conditions and did not allow rehearsals before firing for a score. Only after months of intensive training with the Grand Fleet did the gunnery of the American battleships approach the British standard.

Rear Adm. Hugh Rodman and the members of his staff aboard his flagship the *New York*. Rodman is seated in the center.

The battleship *Texas* (BB-35) at Hampton Roads, Virginia, shortly before the United States entered World War I. The *Texas* joined the American squadron with the Grand Fleet in February 1918. The *Texas* is the only dreadnought battleship left in existence. She is preserved as a monument at the San Jacinto battleground near Houston, Texas.

During World War I aircraft came to play an important role in Allied fleets. They were invaluable for spotting and as scouts. By the end of the war the British were developing carrier aviation and were planning an air raid against the German fleet base. Here a Standard H.S. 2 L. type U.S. naval flying boat flies past the *New York*.

During the King's visit to the Grand Fleet. From left to right: Adm. Sir David Beatty, commander in chief of the British Grand Fleet; Rear Adm. Hugh Rodman, commander of the American squadron with the Grand Fleet; King George V; the Prince of Wales; and Adm. William S. Sims.

The *New York* flying her battle flags during the surrender of the German High Seas Fleet on 21 November 1918. Although not as glamorous as a decisive fleet engagement along classical lines, the German surrender marked an unparalleled naval victory.

Adm. Sir David Beatty greeting Rear Adm. Hugh Rodman beneath the guns of the *Queen Elizabeth*. The spirit of comradeship became the dominant feature of relations between these two remarkable officers. *Imperial War Museum*

The anchorage of U.S. Battleship Division Six at Berehaven, Ireland. The *Nevada* (BB-36), *Oklahoma* (BB-37), and *Utah* (BB-31) moved to Berehaven to protect U.S. troop convoys from German surface raiders. The *Nevada* is in the background.

The *Utah* was the flagship for Rear Adm. Thomas S. Rogers, commander of Battleship Division Six based at Berehaven. The *Utah* is seen here with a sawtooth camouflage pattern along the deck and randomly located sheet metal pennants in the upperworks that made focusing range finders difficult.

The big guns of the *Nevada*. *Nevada* and her sister ship, *Oklahoma*, were the first of a new generation of American battleships featuring "all or nothing" armor protection and the first use of triple turrets. The *Nevada* class concentrated ten 14-inch guns in two triple and two double turrets.

America's newest and most powerful battleships never entered the war zone before the armistice. Seen here is the *New Mexico* (BB-40), completed in May 1918.

Ships of Division Four, Force One, of the Atlantic Fleet under the command of Vice Adm. A. W. Grant. They are cruising in line-abreast during a training exercise. From left to right: probably the *Louisiana* (BB-19); *Kansas* (BB-21); and *New Hampshire* (BB-25). Force One, consisting of the obsolescent pre-dreadnought battleships, served as training ships, convoy escorts, and troop transports during the war. These ships saw duty in the war zone while the most modern U.S. battleships remained in home waters.

The *Kearsarge* (BB-5) was one of the older pre-dreadnoughts and the only battleship not named for a state, but for the Union ship that sank the famed Confederate raider *Alabama*. The *Kearsarge* served as a training vessel during World War I and operated with Force One of the Atlantic Fleet.

The *Nebraska* (BB-14) sporting a camouflage pattern designed to make range finding difficult. The *Nebraska* escorted three troop convoys across the Atlantic between September 1918 and the armistice, and served as a troop transport after the war.

The pre-dreadnought *Vermont* (BB-20) in heavy seas typical of the Atlantic during the stormy months. Besides duty as a training ship, the *Vermont* transported U.S. troops home from France.

4

LESSONS LEARNED

U.S. Naval Gunnery and the Experience
of World War I

✳

In his biography of Adm. William Sims, Elting Morison contended that when Sims left the office of Inspector of Target Practice in 1909, "American gunnery was probably the best in the world."[1] If Morison's contention is true, then in less than a decade, either U.S. gunnery efficiency dramatically declined or British gunnery greatly improved. Upon joining the Grand Fleet, the gunnery of the U.S. battleships could only be considered poor compared to the British.

This poor performance was an unpleasant surprise on both sides of the Atlantic. Adm. Sir David Beatty could not consider the American ships the equivalent of British ships and had to make his plans accordingly. Adm. Hugh Rodman promised the Navy Department that his ships would soon improve and adapt to conditions in the North Sea. But only after months of training with the Grand Fleet did the gunnery of the American battleships finally improve to the point that they were comparable to British battleships. This chapter will examine various factors that contributed to the poor gunnery of the U.S. battleships when they joined the Grand Fleet and to their improvement during service in the war zone.

✳

By the time the First World War began, the development of modern director firing had revolutionized naval gunnery. Since the days of sail, individual gun captains had controlled laying and training the guns. They would fire independently, and a spotter aloft would call corrections. Not only was accuracy subject to the skills of several individuals, but the independent fire made it difficult to know for certain if the gun range was correct.

In 1890 an American naval officer, Lt. (later Rear Adm.) Bradley Fisk, developed and patented the first director firing system. It involved a telescopic sight mounted aloft. The directing officer would sight the target and pass the bearing, elevation, and deflection to the gunners, who would fire on command when the roll of the ship brought the sights on. Fire was under the control of one officer in a commanding position above the interference of smoke and spray.[2]

The problem with the early director firing was the primitive state of existing communications. Director fire became truly practical when British gunnery expert Percy Scott designed a system that used electric transmitters to pass orders from the director to the guns.

Although their officers had pioneered director firing and despite its proven superiority, both the U.S. and British navies were slow to adopt director fire control systems. The Admiralty did not begin installing director systems on British battleships until 1913, and only by the time of the battle of Jutland did most of the ships of the Grand Fleet receive directors for their main armament. The attitude of the U.S. Navy Department toward director firing was even more tepid. The *Texas*, the first U.S. battleship to be fitted with a director system, only received one in the summer of 1916 after it became clear from Jutland that battle would likely be opened at extreme ranges.[3]

The fledgling German navy adopted director firing in 1911, before the U.S. and Britain. However, the Germans used a training director only. Individual gunlayers still sighted the target with their own sights, subject to smoke and spray interference.[4] Furthermore, the Germans failed to perfect any system of plotting the course and speed of enemy ships. For good reason, German gunnery officers placed little reliance on the calculations made in a plotting room.[5]

Most navies by World War I had developed three standard instruments that could predict range. The first was the plotting board, used to graph current enemy positions. The basic data for plotting were successive readings from optical rangefinders, which used triangulation to find the distance to the target. The second instrument was the Dumaresq, which could convert enemy course and speed into the rate the range was changing. In effect this was a mechanical computer, which set up a model of a two-ship engagement. The third instrument was the range clock, on which the range rate could be set, and the changing range read. The base rate could be altered according to spotting information while the clock ran.[6]

Jon Sumida, in his studies of British naval technology, has shown that most fire control systems during World War I failed to calculate the rate of range change accurately. The British Dreyer system, for example, used what amounted to a geometric, or straight-line, approximation to find the solution to what was in fact a differential equation. British inventor Arthur Pollen actually devised a differential analyzer, called the Argo Clock, which produced excellent results, but it was rejected by the Admiralty in favor of the cheaper Dreyer system.[7]

The British fire control system was built around the Vickers director. This director combined multiple functions in a single instrument: it automatically calculated the change in elevation of the directorscope, applied spotting information, and transmitted bearing and elevation data to the guns. The British used the "follow-the-pointer" system, in which the director drove red pointers on the elevation and train dials at the guns. The gunners then simply matched their dials to the pointers.

Deep in the bowels of the ship was a plotting room that housed a Dumaresq mounted on the Dreyer fire control table to generate range and bearing rates. Data from the spotter, rangefinders, and fire control table were all reported to the director. The gunnery officer stationed in the spotting top above the director controlled the whole system.[8] A single key in the director fired all of the main guns simultaneously.

The major difference between the U.S. and British fire control systems was that in the U.S. system the plotting room rather than the director was the brain of the system. The director and rangefinder positions collected and fed range and spotting data to the plotting room. Gunnery officers in the plotting room processed the information and estimated proper bearing and range. They also plotted the trend of the data so they could spot errors. The plotting room then transmitted azimuth and elevation commands to the guns, and finally gave them the order to fire.

The British fire control system was more automated and required fewer personnel, while the U.S. system was more subtle and flexible. For example, it could better divide the fire of one ship between two targets. In theory at least, the U.S. system was also less subject to errors that would have a great impact on a more automated system. The U.S. system, with its emphasis on plotting, was more likely to detect range and deflection errors than the British system. For the U.S. system to pay off, however, it demanded highly trained personnel. The U.S. system placed great responsibility on spotters and officers in the plotting room.[9]

The only feature of the British fire control system the gunnery officers of the U.S. squadron with the Grand Fleet considered superior was the follow-the-pointer system for gunlaying and training. In U.S. battleships, electric counters in the turrets gave the elevation only. This process required several operators to read actual figures from one instrument and remember them while transferring them to another instrument. The gunnery officers considered this system "awkward, slow, inaccurate under favorable conditions, and liable to be fatally so in the stress of battle."[10] In 1917, the U.S. Navy began installing a follow-the-pointer system to indicate train, but did not provide that system for elevation until late 1918.[11]

One important strength of the U.S. system was that the Sperry fire control system included a device similar to Pollen's Argo Clock called the Ford Rangekeeper, an analog computer that could also solve differential equations. This instrument could generate predicted ranges, but not predicted bearings. Bearings had to be plotted manually on the Mark II plotting board. A future commander of the Seventh Fleet in World War II, Lt. Cdr. Thomas C. Kinkaid, visited the Grand Fleet in February 1918 to compare U.S. and British gunnery and recommended the Ford Rangekeeper be modified to predict bearing.[12] This was accomplished in 1926.[13]

As early as February 1914 the U.S. Bureau of Ordnance considered the Pollen system but rejected it on account of its mechanical complexity and expense. The bureau admitted that the Pollen devices were "very ingenious and interesting," but cited the British Admiralty's failure to adopt the system as substantiation of their decision.[14] During the summer of 1917, however, the bureau reversed its decision and recommended purchasing a set of Pollen instruments for trial. The chief of the Bureau of Ordnance, Rear Adm. Ralph Earle, concluded that "the United States Navy cannot afford not to be in possession of these instruments."[15]

In November 1917 Pollen learned of the similarity of the Ford Rangekeeper to his device and complained to the Bureau of Ordnance about the infringement of his patent rights. The bureau assured Pollen that Ford had conceived this invention completely independently of any information about the Pollen clock and before some of Pollen's patents had been issued.[16] Pollen admitted that he was basing the charge on secondhand information and said he considered it a misunderstanding.[17]

The bureau then contracted with Pollen's company for one Argo Clock and plotter, which was installed on the *Louisiana* in June 1918 and tested while the ship was on convoy duty. The officers of the *Louisiana* reported that the Argo Clock and the Ford Rangekeeper were equally accurate, but the Pollen system was much easier to operate and maintain. They reported that they had "considerably more confidence" in the Pollen than the Ford.[18] Nevertheless, the Bureau of Ordnance decided that the Argo did not have enough advantages over the Rangekeeper to warrant the fleet adopting it.[19]

Operations in the North Sea revealed design problems that affected the gunnery of U.S. battleships. Several officers noticed that U.S. battleships had much more motion than British battleships, and consequently were poorer gun platforms. Rodman recommended that the Navy Department consider improving the stability of the U.S. battleships, noting that the *New York* and *Texas* had the most motion, the *Wyoming* and *Arkansas* somewhat less, and the *Florida* had still less motion. The exact cause of the motion was never determined.[20]

Another problem was the location of the rangefinders. Severe weather in the North Sea rendered rangefinders on the forward turrets all but useless. Spray clouded the optics and the observers had no weather protection. High winds could even blow an observer off the turret.

In February 1918, Admiral Rodman recommended that the forward rangefinder be moved above the fire control tower.[21] In August, he reported that during recent operations in the North Sea, so much water came aboard that none of the rangefinders in the ship could operate for a time, and recommended that the department follow the British practice of moving rangefinders above the foretops. Neither recommendation was immediately acted upon, but although they remained poorly positioned, the U.S. long-based rangefinders were still superior to British rangefinders, which had shorter bases. After seeing the performance of American rangefinders, the Admiralty began acquiring long-based rangefinders.[22]

Design problems also affected the torpedo-defense guns. The secondary batteries in the lower decks had proven to be wet even before the war, but conditions in the North Sea made them inoperable. Rodman reported that aboard the *New York*, during a four-day cruise, the weather was calm enough to man the lower-deck guns on only one day. On the other three days, only two 5-inch guns in open mounts could operate.[23] Likewise, the captain of the *Texas* recalled that during his entire wartime service he could rarely use the lower-deck guns and he only manned two of the open 5-inch guns while at sea. The Navy Department began removing hull-mounted secondary guns from battleships during the war, but the U.S. battleships with the Grand Fleet did not remove any of theirs until after the war.[24]

*

One of the reasons for the poor gunnery of U.S. battleships when they joined the Grand Fleet was the shortage of experienced officers and men. Following its practice in other American wars, the United States did not mobilize its manpower until after the declaration of war. The total strength of the U.S. Navy was 67,000 officers and men when the war began; by the end of the war, the Navy's ranks had swelled to nearly a half-million.

Training programs could not keep pace with such a rapid expansion.[25] As many as 75 percent of the enlisted men in the gunnery divisions on some ships had less than a year's experience.[26] The decision to remove experienced gunners from battleships to man guns on merchant ships further depleted the cadre of trained men. Admiral Rodman recalled that he had only enough crews for half of his ships' secondary batteries when the war began. In battle, he would have had to shift all of the gun crews to the engaged side only. The Navy Department brought Rodman's battleships up to strength just prior to their departure for Europe, but according to Rodman, "They gave us a lot of recruits that were not trained."[27]

Rodman listed changes in, and inexperience of, personnel as a major reason for the poor showing his ships made at their first full-caliber firing in European waters. Rodman suggested at the time that he could eliminate the deficiencies if the department would not make any further changes in personnel.[28] Several months later, Rodman made the same point, but more forcefully:

> All Officers we have at present have been assigned important battle stations and our increasing efficiency is largely due to our permanency in personnel. It is not desired that officers trained elsewhere be sent to replace those already in the division, for no matter how efficient they may be, any appreciable change of personnel is bound to disrupt a ship's organization. It is most earnestly recommended that no more reserve officers be sent to this division for training and that we no longer be considered available for training purposes.[29]

Rodman also complained about the loss of his divisional gunnery officer, Cdr. Husband E. Kimmel, who would later become commander in chief of the Pacific Fleet and then be forced into retirement after the debacle at Pearl Harbor. The Navy Department had ordered Kimmel home on 30 January 1918, but sent him back to Rodman's command in July. Kimmel's absence was a hardship because no other officer could spare the time from regular work to take over the duties of a full-time divisional gunnery officer, which included not only improving divisional gunnery but also studying and assimilating the good points of British methods and policy.[30]

The commander in chief of the Atlantic Fleet, Adm. Henry Mayo, and his staff inspected the U.S. squadron with the Grand Fleet for four days in early September 1918. Mayo agreed with the conclusion that the gunnery efficiency of the force had suffered because of the rapid expansion of the Navy and consequent reduction of officers and transfers of large numbers of the crews. He also stated that the lack of a permanent divisional gunnery officer had retarded the development of gunnery efficiency.[31] In addition, Mayo reported that officers of the Sixth Battle Squadron had expressed their belief that detaching officers and men not only hurt efficiency but also morale. They called attention to the fact that reliefs were often not available to fill their places and that the leadership should make provisions to avoid such a situation in the future.[32]

✳

Perhaps the most valuable benefit to the U.S. Navy of service with the Grand Fleet was the realization that U.S. training methods left much to be desired and the resultant emulation of British methods, developed during the war. The British worked hard to hold target practices under actual war conditions. Based on experience in battle, the Grand Fleet added difficulties and limitations to their practices that would simulate problems they would likely encounter in battle.[33] U-boats and mines infested the area where the Grand Fleet practiced. Just prior to each practice, it was necessary for minesweepers to clear the range and lanes of approach. By contrast, the Atlantic Fleet held their target practices only in favorable weather conditions and on a previously determined range. Furthermore, U.S. practice allowed rehearsals and practice runs before firing for a score. The British system did not allow second chances. Time and the limited protected space negated any practice approach. Besides, the conditions of the practice simply mirrored reality—second chances are few in actual combat.[34]

The U.S. battle practice procedures had been developed before modern fire control. The practices were based on competition between ships, the primary purpose being to train and qualify gun pointers. The problem with this form of practice was that pointer fire was only an auxiliary system by World War I, yet the skills of the pointers were still being emphasized over development of the fire control party.[35] Admiral Sims, who had championed the competitive system while he was inspector of target practice, remained committed to the system as late as 1916. In a letter to Sims analyzing the implications of the battle of Jutland, a lieutenant, J. H. Klein, had the temerity to suggest that British and German long-range gunnery was superior to U.S. gunnery. Klein suggested that increasing battle practice ranges would improve efficiency. Sims responded with a forceful memorandum circulated at the Naval War College, in which he characterized Klein's conclusions as "erroneous" and "extremely dangerous as a guide to future battle training." He bristled at the idea that European shooting was superior and he defended the short-range battle practice as the only way to determine the errors of individual pointers. The first requirement of accurate gunnery, Sims contended, was reliable pointing.[36]

Criticism of U.S. battle practices increased after the American squadron joined the Grand Fleet. Following his visit to the Grand Fleet in February 1918, Admiral Kinkaid made one of the first endorsements of British training methods. He recommended that all U.S. gunnery training be done at sea and in division formation, with frequent course changes and at maximum speed. He also suggested the U.S. Navy develop fire concentration, as the British had.[37]

The first full-caliber practice in the war zone by the *Texas*, holder of the gunnery trophy, provoked Admiral Rodman, too, to criticize the system of gunnery training in the U.S. Navy. He noted that practice in the Grand Fleet was based on a "*war* and not necessarily on a *competitive* basis," and stated that the recent practices of the *Texas* and the other ships of the squadron illustrated their unpreparedness. He asserted that their poor shooting was "a commentary on our system wherein rehearsals, special grooming, and a cut and dried program seems to be expected before a ship can make hits and make them rapidly." Rodman emphasized that the *Texas* was not the exception, "but rather a glaring generality, and if all our vessels are as poorly prepared as these were, to actually go into action on short notice, some change should be made in our system."[38]

During his testimony in 1920 before the Senate Subcommittee on Naval Affairs, which was investigating the Navy Department's conduct of the war, Rodman changed his tune. He minimized his earlier criticism of U.S. gunnery training, referring to it as "trifling." Rodman related that he had perceived that the *Texas* was "still focused on winning the pennant," and that he told the officers "to get over that competition business." Rodman testified that his criticism only referred to the *Texas* and no other battleships. He went so far as to state, "The rest of the ships were excellent, but the *Texas* was rotten when she arrived." Rodman's testimony clearly contradicts his general reports to the Navy Department. It seems likely that he was very anxious to defend the Navy Department against Sims and other critics. Admitting that U.S. gunnery was inefficient when hostilities began would have given critics a powerful weapon.[39]

The Navy Department did embrace British training methods by the time the war ended, and U.S. gunnery improved as a result. Atlantic Fleet exercises in 1918 still included an individual ship practice with a rehearsal run, but it was carried out in unfavorable conditions and at top speed with frequent course changes. More important was the introduction of division practices that included fire-concentration problems and multiple targets.[40] In 1921 the Navy Department introduced fleet fire-concentration exercises, with as many as fourteen battleships firing on twelve targets according to concentration rules. The fleet also used aircraft for spotting.[41]

Although the battle practices became more complex and the ranges increased each year during the early twenties, so did the number of shots and hits per gun per minute. In 1919 at a range of over 15,500 yards the average performance for all battleships was .880 shots per minute per gun and .099 hits per minute per gun. In 1922 the practice range had increased to over 19,000 yards, with .933 shots per gun per minute and .104 hits per gun per minute. As the ranges increased, so did the fire control difficulties—yet gunnery improved.[42]

By 1925 the fleet had taken great strides to simulate war conditions. Commenting on the fleet gunnery exercises that year during a lecture at the Naval War College, Cdr. Henry Hewitt, who became commander of the Eighth Fleet during World War II, recognized that gunnery practices had been held under "artificial conditions" for many years. Hewitt reported that during the 1925 force practice, the battle line fired its main, secondary, and antiaircraft batteries while maneuvering to avoid a torpedo attack by destroyers. He proclaimed that the only thing lacking to simulate an actual engagement was high-speed targets.[43] In the years after World War I, U.S. gunnery practices advanced from little more than matches between ships to fleet gunnery exercises that spurred the improvement of long-range gunnery and fire control.

*

The most common British complaint against American gunnery was the excessive spread of the patterns of their main battery broadsides. In a report to the Admiralty following his visit to the Atlantic Fleet soon after the United States entered the war, Cdr. Richard Down, R.N., noted that American battleships averaged spreads of over 800 yards. He proposed three reasons for these excessive spreads: weak turret mountings, excessive muzzle pressures owing to high muzzle velocity, and the American practice of firing double-barrel salvos.[44] The British used single-barrel salvos because they only had sufficient power in their turrets to load one gun at a time. After the war the British increased the power in their turrets and began firing double-barrel salvos.[45]

The American squadron's first full-caliber firing with the Grand Fleet achieved an average pattern for the squadron of 757 yards—average for

U.S. battleships, but poor by British standards.[46] After observing this practice, Admiral Kinkaid pronounced large patterns "the most vital gunnery problem before us today." He recommended that the Navy Department take drastic measures to solve the problem "at the earliest possible moment." Kinkaid suggested assigning one battleship with unlimited ammunition devoted solely to reducing the patterns. Considering there was a war on, and that prolonged firing would wear the tubes, this was a drastic step. The Navy Department did not resort to Kinkaid's suggestion, but did begin studying the problem. Nearly a decade would pass before the Navy Department would be able to isolate the principal cause of the large patterns.[47]

At its 15 October practice, the U.S. squadron reduced their average spread to 600 yards.[48] A little over two weeks previously, at a full-caliber practice of the Second Battle Squadron, the *Erin, Agincourt, Orion,* and *Conqueror* had patterns that averaged 572 yards. This was a larger-than-average pattern for the British, whose spreads were usually 300 yards for a single-barrel salvo and 400 yards for a double-barrel salvo. It should also be pointed out that at this same practice of the Second Battle Squadron, there were rangefinding errors, communication failures, and numerous other deficiencies. The British evidently had bad days too. The Americans, however, never did consistently achieve patterns that were as small as the British average.[49]

By all accounts, the gunnery of the American squadron improved significantly while serving with the Grand Fleet. One indication of its efficiency is a comment by the British commander of the ship that towed the target for all Grand Fleet practices. Following a full-caliber practice of the Sixth Squadron in July, he told Rodman that he had never witnessed better firing than that of the American squadron. Rodman recorded this praise in his general report and added, "This is not only gratifying but shows that our methods of training, our installations, and fire control and personnel, are at least equal if not superior to the British."[50] Rodman may have been overly exuberant about the praise of a single British officer, but the fact remains that the Americans' shooting had improved to the point that it was gaining notice and praise.

Although gunnery improved during the war, excessive patterns continued to bedevil U.S. battleships during the 1920s. At the long-range practice in 1923, some battleships had patterns that exceeded 2,000 yards! It was becoming clear that some classes of ships consistently had large patterns. In a Naval War College lecture on gunnery that year, Capt. R. M. Brainard summed up the seriousness of the excessive patterns:

> There is no doubt, in my opinion, that much thought must be given to this matter if we expect any hits on straddles. To me, this is one of the most important things in gunnery that must be solved and unless we do, I am afraid we cannot expect the hitting power that we need in order to defeat an equal force as to number of guns.[51]

As head of the gunnery section in the Division of Fleet Training, Commander Hewitt's lecture on gunnery developments for 1925 at the Naval War College reported that there seemed to be no solution to the problem of dispersion. An analysis of the long-range firings for the last eight years had shown no improvement. Interestingly, certain classes of ships had consistently bad patterns for the entire period. The best gun was the new 16-inch/45 caliber, which had very small patterns. The next best was the 12-inch/45 caliber (*Delaware* class), followed by the 14-inch/45 caliber gun (*New York* class through *Pennsylvania* class). The 12-inch/50 caliber guns (*Wyoming* class) were the worst. (It should be remembered that the *Wyoming* and *Florida* had suffered the most excessive patterns of the battleships in the American squadron with the Grand Fleet.) The 14-inch/50 caliber (*California* class) was the only inconsistent performer, achieving very small patterns at 18,000 yards but the largest patterns of all at 25,000 yards. The problem of dispersion, then, was clearly not a matter of personnel performance, but of flaws inherent in the particular type of gun.[52] The problem was no closer to a solution, but the Navy had finally narrowed down the main cause.

There were a number of factors that account for the poor gunnery of the U.S. battleships when they joined the Grand Fleet. Only after months of intensive training in war conditions did the gunnery of the American battleships approach the British standard. By the end of the war, the overall gunnery efficiency of the American battleships was almost equivalent to that of the British. The problem of excessive patterns, however, continued to plague the U.S. Navy for the next decade.

5

DEFENDING THE TRANSATLANTIC CONVOYS

Planning for a Possible Battle Cruiser Raid,
May to October 1918

✳

The most important contribution of the U.S. Navy during World War I was to transport over two million American troops to Europe, the decisive theater. General Erich Ludendorff's spring offensive, which coincided with the American troop buildup, was a race against time to defeat the war-weary Allied armies before the United States could throw its sword into the balance. American naval leaders never doubted that the war would be won or lost on the Western Front.

Chief of Naval Operations Adm. William Benson placed priority on protecting U.S. troop convoys, rather than on guarding the U.S. coast or supplying escort for mercantile convoys.[1] Benson realized that the American troop convoys presented the Imperial German Navy with an opportunity to affect the outcome of the war. He further realized that, although submarines were the principal danger to the convoys, there was also the possibility that one or more German battle cruisers would escape into the Atlantic, and the only way to guard the troop convoys against such powerful raiders would be to protect them with battleships.

✳

The success of the three German commerce raiders, the *Moewe, Wolf,* and *Seeadler,* in late 1916 and early 1917, combined with the decreasing effectiveness of the U-boats, made the increased use of raiders more likely.[2] All of Germany's commerce raiders until that time had been auxiliary warships, but Admiralty planners began worrying about the use of German battle cruisers as convoy raiders as early as November 1917.

The auxiliary warship raiders had always followed the coast of Norway to escape from the North Sea. It was improbable that auxiliary warships would attempt the southern exit from the North Sea, but enemy battle cruisers might force the Dover Straits and attack the convoy approach routes to the English Channel.[3] The Plans Division proposed that the Admiralty base a number of capital ships on the channel to intercept these potential raiders before they escaped into the open Atlantic. They suggested that either the French or the Japanese might be able to spare ships for this purpose, but the Admiralty took no action on their proposal. The Dover mine barrage would have to suffice.[4]

On 17 December 1917, the Admiralty contacted the American chief of naval operations to relate their anxiety about providing "more effective protection for troop convoys from Halifax against possible enemy surface raiders." The Admiralty proposed to use two large cruisers for this purpose: the *Leviathan* and the *King Alfred*, both launched in 1901. They contended that they had no more resources to offer, but because U.S. troops were involved, they suggested that the U.S. Navy Department might detail four pre-dreadnoughts for escort duty.[5]

The next day, Adm. William Sims cabled Benson to explain that the Admiralty's proposal was in response to his earlier suggestion that, because of the presence of U.S. troops, only the largest cruisers should escort the Halifax convoys. He recommended that, because of the harsh winter weather and speed of the convoys, the department should wait until spring before considering the use of the pre-dreadnoughts, which would not be able to maintain sufficient speed to escort the convoys in the heavy weather of winter, not to mention having very poor crew conditions in rough seas.[6] Benson answered that the department had decided to order two armored cruisers to Halifax to work with the British cruisers. These cruisers would be able to fend off the average German commerce raider, but would be no match for a battle cruiser. Nevertheless, there were no immediate plans to use any of the pre-dreadnoughts to escort convoys.[7]

It was not until the American troop convoys began crossing the Atlantic in large numbers that naval planners decided that additional steps were necessary. They developed a series of plans to protect the troop convoys, and those plans continued to evolve until the end of the war. Producing a plan that was acceptable to both the Admiralty Plans Division and the American planning section—one that both the Admiralty and Navy Department would approve—proved to be an arduous process.[8]

Sometime in May 1918, the Admiralty drew up a proposed plan of action to counter potential battle cruiser raids. The plan called for U.S. battleships to escort the troop transports and convoys sailing from Halifax and New York. The Grand Fleet would intercept any raiders on their return journey from hunting convoys in the North Atlantic. British battle cruisers, however, would not hunt for any raiders in the open Atlantic unless very good intelligence became available.[9]

The American planning section, which worked in conjunction with the Admiralty Plans Division, submitted their own plan for consideration. The Americans stressed that the accelerated delivery of U.S. troops would have an important impact on the military situation on the Western Front, and they pointed out that "this fact cannot but be known to the enemy and may therefore cause him to take extraordinary measures to interrupt the supply of men from America." Unlike the Plans Division memorandum of November 1917, the American planning section considered the northern route to be the most likely course of enemy battle cruisers because fuel ships and scouting submarines could accompany them. To protect the convoys, they suggested that one modern U.S. battleship escort each important troop convoy. Even though a battle cruiser's guns could outrange a pre-dreadnought's, the planning section considered that two pre-dreadnoughts were sufficient for escort if a modern battleship was unavailable. The planning section also recommended that additional battle cruisers be conveniently stationed to intercept any enemy battle cruiser. They suggested that a Japanese battle cruiser division could transfer to European waters for that purpose.[10]

In early July, Benson's anxiety about the safety of the troop convoys prompted him to remind Sims of the danger and that the Navy Department depended upon him for prompt information so they could take action if any German battle cruisers escaped into the Atlantic.[11] Sims answered that the Grand Fleet was ready to act against any German raiders, but that it was impossible to guarantee that enemy battle cruisers would not gain the open ocean. Referring to the planning section memorandum, Sims stated that only the provision of battleships for escorts could ensure the safety of the troop convoys.[12]

✳

In late July the Navy Department proposed its own plan for protecting the troop convoys. This plan was similar to the planning section's proposal in several respects: The Navy Department plan also assumed that enemy battle cruisers would use the northern exit, endorsed the use of Japanese battle cruisers for pursuit, and would provide two pre-dreadnoughts to escort each important troop convoy. However, the Navy Department plan went into greater detail than previous plans.

According to the Navy Department plan, Division Six of the Atlantic Fleet, consisting of the coal-burner *Utah* and the oil-burners *Nevada* and *Oklahoma*, would be stationed at Queenstown, Ireland, or Brest, France. Division Eight, consisting of the newest battleships, *Arizona, New Mexico*, and *Pennsylvania*, would remain with the Atlantic Fleet, but would be available to help cover the western Atlantic.[13]

The department proposed to divide the North Atlantic into three zones: the Western Atlantic, from the U.S. coast to 45° west longitude; the Mid-Atlantic, from 45° to 20° west longitude; and the Eastern Atlantic, from 20° west longitude to Europe. In the event an enemy battle cruiser were to escape into the Atlantic, all eastbound convoys in the western zone would return to U.S. or Canadian ports, those in the middle zone would divert to the Azores, and convoys in the eastern zone would proceed to their destination or the nearest port. In the case of westbound convoys, those between Europe and 15° west longitude would either return to port or divert to the Azores, those between 15° and 45° west longitude would divert to the Azores or proceed to the nearest U.S. or Canadian port, and convoys in the western zone would proceed to their destination. Division Six would steam at top speed to the Azores to protect the shipping there, while Division Eight would be ready to proceed where needed.[14] Meanwhile, the Japanese battle cruisers would begin their hunt. The plan would not go into operation until the department gained information that a raider had escaped.[15]

Neither Sims nor the Admiralty was satisfied with the Navy Department's plan. Sims, having apparently lost his earlier faith in British naval intelligence, strongly objected to the plan's reliance on it: "I believe that it is extremely dangerous to base a plan on assumption that information of enemy's escape will be otherwise than through news of an attack." In his view, the department should assume the worst—that one or more enemy battle cruisers would gain the open Atlantic with ample fuel before the Allies detected them. Sims stressed that the only way to protect the convoys was regular battleship escort before the danger arose. He also objected to the assembly of so much shipping in the Azores during an alarm, pointing out the danger to them of submarine attack and the inevitable refueling difficulties. Sims proposed that a better use of battleships at Queenstown or Brest would be to meet important troop convoys at sea and escort them to safety rather than having these convoys proceed unescorted to the Azores. He concluded by reminding Admiral Benson that any final plan should be a joint undertaking with the British.[16]

The Admiralty Plans Division objected to the division of the Atlantic into three zones and the "hard-and-fast" nature of the Navy Department's instructions. They argued that these instructions would not leave enough discretion to the officers of convoys, who would be better placed to make judgments concerning the convoy's safety. In addition, the plan would unnecessarily dislocate the whole convoy system in the North Atlantic. The interruption in troop and cargo movements would be serious.[17] The Admiralty also objected to basing a plan on the assumption that British naval intelligence could give advance warning that an enemy battle cruiser had escaped from the North Sea. Like Sims, the Admiralty was of the opinion that battleships should escort the troop convoys on a regular basis.[18]

The Plans Division drafted another, more detailed, set of plans as a counterproposal to the Navy Department's plan. According to this plan, neither the Admiralty nor the Navy Department would direct traffic during a battle cruiser raid. Instead, convoy officers would be able to choose from a series of optional strategies: rendezvous at friendly ports; proceed to their destination, relying on dodging the raider or scattering the convoy as a last resort; or alter course or speed to avoid the danger area until the raider had withdrawn. The plan listed three basic principles to guide the convoy officers on which course to take: because of the poor odds that the patrolling forces would find the raider on the open sea, convoy vessels should rely on their own efforts; they should expect a raiding battle cruiser to cooperate with U-boats; and since any delay in the arrival of the convoy was a serious disadvantage, convoy officers should accept reasonable risks.[19]

A beneficial feature of the Plans Division paper was an appendix predicting probable movements of a raiding battle cruiser. This included a

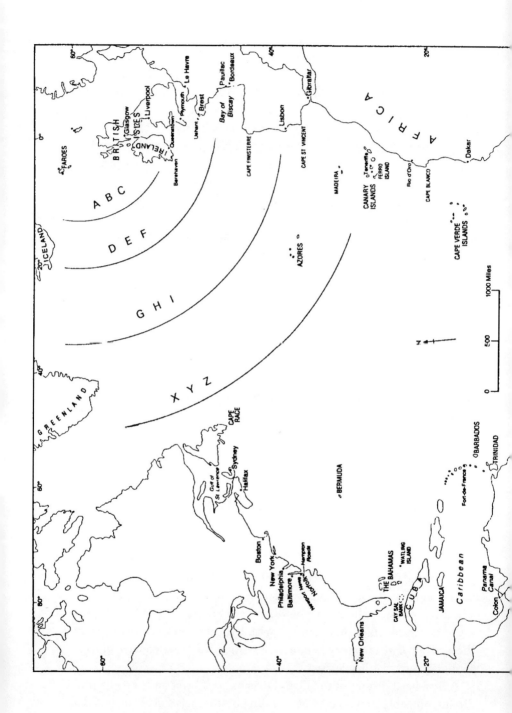

diagram showing the limits of the *Derfflinger*'s endurance based on estimated fuel consumption. The *Derfflinger* was one of Germany's newest
battle cruisers. A third of her boilers could burn oil, so she could extend
her range if she captured an oiler. Because fueling at sea at that time was
dangerous and required good weather, however, the planners concluded
that it would not be an essential feature of the German plan, and so was
more likely to extend the duration rather than the field of the raider's
operations.

On the Plans Division's diagram, the line XYZ showed the extreme
limit of the *Derfflinger*'s range if the vessel took a direct route at economical speed. The battle cruiser could operate at lines GHI for two days,
DEF for four days, and ABC for six days. The purpose of this diagram was
to assist in selecting a route for the convoy which would be safe if the enemy battle cruiser did not refuel.[20]

*

On 12 August, the *Nevada* and *Oklahoma* of Division Six, under the
command of Rear Adm. Thomas S. Rodgers, left Hampton Roads for
Berehaven, Ireland. The *Utah* would join the division at the end of the
month, following an overhaul at the Norfolk Navy Yard.[21]

Upon learning that Rodgers had sailed for European waters, Sims sent
him a personal letter of welcome, along with the Navy Department's instructions. Sims volunteered his low opinion of the Navy Department's
plan, indicating that he was working to have those plans changed. In particular, he expressed his belief that basing the plan on the presumption
that there would be advance warning of a battle cruiser's escape was "a
dangerous assumption."[22]

(*Facing page*) The vulnerability of American troop convoys to powerful raiders such as
battle cruisers presented the German navy with an opportunity to affect the outcome
of the war. The Navy Department countered the threat by providing battleship escorts. This map shows the limits of a raiding battle cruiser's endurance based on estimated fuel consumption. Line XYZ is the extreme limit at economical speed. A raider
could operate at line GHI for two days, line DEF for four days, and line ABC for six
days. *Adaptation of the map "The North Atlantic" in Halpern's* A Naval History of World War I,
page 458.

On 31 August 1918, the Navy Department implemented its plan as far as the diversion of routes was concerned. Benson also announced that the department would begin providing battleship escort for the HX and HC convoys, which were mixed mercantile and troop convoys from New York and Halifax, respectively, and also for the U.S. Navy's own troop convoys. U.S. pre-dreadnoughts would perform this service, beginning on 9 September. The department would put the entire plan into operation if there was information of the escape of a raider.[23]

Sims responded to Benson's announcement, saying that the Admiralty did not wish to divert the HX and HC convoys to the Azores. One or more of the battleships at Berehaven could escort those convoys. Sims instructed Rodgers that the diversion plan would remain in effect for the U.S. troop and HB convoys from New York.[24] The HB convoy, which supplied U.S. troops in France, had French armored cruisers as part of its escort.[25]

Benson complained that the Admiralty's "disinclination" to divert the HX and HC convoys according to the Navy Department's plan weakened it because the U.S. Navy would have to strengthen the escort for those convoys, since they also carried U.S. troops. Benson approved Sims's suggestion that battleships from Division Six escort the HX and HC convoys in the event of a raider warning, but on the condition that at least one of them protect the troop convoys diverted to the Azores. He stated that because no joint agreement had been reached, only U.S. ships would receive the Navy Department's plan. The U.S. pre-dreadnoughts escorting the HX and HC convoys would have a copy of the plan, but would not use it unless the Admiralty desired to use it.

The chief of naval operations recognized that the Navy Department's plan was only a temporary expedient. Although troop convoys were being protected, cargo convoys were still vulnerable. Furthermore, there were no provisions for a pursuit division. Even the most modern dreadnoughts were too slow to catch a battle cruiser, and neither the British nor the Japanese were willing to detach any of their battle cruisers for this purpose.[26]

The next attempt to achieve an acceptable plan was a proposal prepared jointly by the Admiralty Plans Division and the American planning section. Although a joint undertaking, this plan heavily favored British priorities. It followed the premise that to make the best use of the available forces, the protection of *all* Allied convoys, not just the troop convoys, should constitute a single problem. Although the plan advocated that the troop convoys take precedence, it would have extended battleship protection to mercantile cargoes as well, which was never the Navy Department's intention. In addition, any plan should also involve similar instructions from both the Admiralty and the Navy Department.

The joint plan repeated the British criticism of issuing "hard-and-fast" instructions. Instead of diverting convoys out of the danger zone during a raid, it emphasized that "every effort must be made as soon as possible to provide with adequate escorts all convoys likely to pass through dangerous areas." The plan also suggested the awkward expedient of dividing operational control of the convoys between the Admiralty and the Navy Department. The former would control the convoys east of 45° west longitude, while the latter would control those to the west.

In the event of a raider warning, the unescorted eastbound convoys would rendezvous with battleships from Berehaven before proceeding, while convoys with battleship escorts from Halifax would continue. Eastbound convoys to the east of the probable position of the raider would continue unescorted. Westbound convoys to the east of a raider would return to the nearest port, while those to the west would continue. If the raider was in the western Atlantic, battleships from Hampton Roads or Halifax would meet the westbound convoys. The purpose of this routing was to keep the maximum amount of shipping moving toward their destinations, rather than diverting shipping and losing valuable time. This plan assumed that if the HC, HX, and U.S. troop convoys already had their own battleship escorts, three battleships at Berehaven and one to three at Halifax would suffice for the other convoys. If the troop convoys were not already provided with regular battleship escorts, then the United States would have to provide an additional three battleships for Berehaven and five at Halifax.[27]

＊

The Admiralty and the Navy Department finally reached an agreement on a joint plan to protect the convoys from a battle cruiser raid as the result of conferences at the Navy Department on 9 and 10 October, during a visit of First Lord Sir Eric Geddes. At the conferences, Capt. C. T.

M. Fuller of the Plans Division represented the Admiralty and Capt. William Veazie Pratt represented the Navy Department. This final plan, known as "Plan BCR," closely resembled the joint plan of the Admiralty Plans Division and American planning section. Ultimately, the Navy Department made significant concessions to the British in order to achieve a joint agreement.

Plan BCR contained no provisions for diverting convoys to the Azores or anywhere else. Avoiding shipping delays was one of the guiding principles of the plan. In addition, it provided protection for both troop convoys and purely mercantile ones. The plan entailed committing a substantial number of heavy ships for escorts. It estimated a need for thirty-five pre-dreadnoughts or armored cruisers. The United States would provide twenty-four of these: fourteen pre-dreadnoughts and ten armored cruisers. Britain would supply seven pre-dreadnoughts, which would be manned by U.S. Navy crews, along with four armored cruisers with British crews. In terms of dreadnoughts, the Navy Department would increase the number of battleships at Berehaven to four and would station three dreadnoughts at Halifax. Following a raider warning, the battleships at Berehaven would meet the troop convoys that were east of 40° west longitude, and the battleships at Halifax would proceed where needed. The Navy Department would most likely recall any troop convoys west of 40° west longitude and use the Halifax dreadnoughts to support the cargo convoys.

Like the earlier joint plan, Plan BCR divided control of the Atlantic convoys between the Admiralty and the Navy Department. This plan, however, divided spheres of action by time instead of convoy position, because it would often be impossible to know exactly when a convoy had crossed a particular longitude. According to the final plan, before each convoy sailed, an estimated time of crossing 40° west longitude, designated "time A," was assigned to that convoy. In the event of a raider warning, any convoy with a time A later than the time given in the warning would come under the control of the Navy Department; those with an earlier time A would come under the control of the Admiralty. Plan BCR differed from previous plans in that it included no special provisions for westbound convoys. The above instructions applied to eastbound convoys only. Westbound shipping would proceed independently after dispersal from the outward convoys, which only provided antisubmarine escorts in the U-boat danger zone.[28]

Agreement on a joint Anglo-American plan to counter the threat of a possible German battle cruiser raid against the troop convoys took as long to negotiate as the later Treaty of Versailles. After six long months of negotiations, the Admiralty and the Navy Department had finally agreed on a joint plan of operations to protect the convoys from a battle cruiser raid, only to have the war end before they could fully implement it. No German battle cruisers ever sortied against the troop convoys, and the preparations to counter a raid were not needed.

The fact remains that the Germans *could* have used their powerful battle cruisers against the troop convoys. They had shown their ability to sortie their entire battle fleet undetected. The German battle cruisers almost certainly could have escaped into the Atlantic. Even the logistical problems of such a raid were not insurmountable. Most of the Allied naval leadership agreed that a battle cruiser raid was a real possibility. Perhaps some of them doubted the Germans would attack the convoys, but they all understood the prudence of prevention.

In spite of their agreement in principle on providing better protection for the valuable and vulnerable troop convoys, the Admiralty and the Navy Department took many months to agree on a joint plan of action. Only after the Navy department was willing to accommodate British views and priorities did a joint effort become possible. This is yet another illustration of the difficulty of naval cooperation between the two allies during World War I.

6

SENTINELS

Battleship Division Six at Berehaven,

August to November 1918

✻

Because of the possibility that one or more German battle cruisers might slip out to sea and assail Allied convoys in the Atlantic, the Navy Department decided to send Battleship Division Six of the Atlantic Fleet to Berehaven, Ireland. Berehaven, on Bantry Bay, was situated close to the shipping lanes between the United States and ports in France and southern Britain. It was also close to Queenstown, Ireland, where most of America's destroyers were stationed, making it an ideal location for a base from which the battleships could guard the convoys.

✻

On 12 August 1918, the *Nevada*, commanded by Capt. A. T. Long, and the *Oklahoma*, under Capt. Mark Bristol, sailed from the fleet anchorage at Hampton Roads for Berehaven, Ireland. Rear Adm. Thomas Rodgers flew his flag on *Nevada* until his flagship, the *Utah*, could finish her overhaul and rejoin the division. The division enjoyed a calm and uneventful passage, arriving at Berehaven at 1840 on 23 August. The next day, the U.S. oiler *Frank S. Buck* fueled the ships to capacity, and the division was ready for duty.[1]

Rodgers was from a famous naval family, and he was known as a salty character. Vice Adm. John McCrea, who had served with Rodgers before the war, recalled him fondly: "I liked Rodgers very much. He was a bachelor. He was a cigar-smoker. He was profane." Rodgers also had "a low boiling point." McCrea recounted a story of the day Rodgers, then a captain, resolved to stop swearing. Pacing across the bridge puffing on his cigar he declared: "I've made up my mind not to swear today, not even once." But before the day was over, a noisy chipping hammer began to grate on the captain's nerves. Finally, Rodgers wheeled on the officer of the deck: "G——d—— it, Mr. Comfort! Stop that g——d—— chipping hammer from making all that racket!" Then, with a faint smile, Rodgers said, "Now, there it goes. I wasn't going to swear today, and since I have already sworn today, there is no use in my not swearing more today if I want to. I'll try not to swear tomorrow and see how it goes."[2]

Two of Rodgers's battleships were among the most modern (the *Utah* was one of the older *Florida*-class ships). The *Nevada* and *Oklahoma* were the first of a new generation of U.S. battleships. These two sister ships introduced a revolutionary design: "all-or-nothing" protection. Since armor-piercing shells did not burst when penetrating thin, splinter armor, there was nothing to gain from using thin armor. The designers chose to provide either the thickest armor, which shells could not penetrate, on the vital areas of the ship, or no armor at all. Reflecting the demands of increasing gunnery ranges, the all-or-nothing arrangement saved weight, allowing the designers to increase the deck armor to protect against plunging fire. The *Nevada* class also introduced the triple turret, which saved weight by concentrating ten 14-inch/45 caliber guns into two triple turrets and two double turrets, rather than in five double turrets as on the *New York* class. The *Nevada*-class ships were also the first oil-fueled U.S. battleships.[3]

Unlike Division Nine, which was serving with the Grand Fleet as the Sixth Battle Squadron, Division Six was not under British operational control. Rodgers could not exercise command over any British naval forces, nor could any British officer exercise command over any part of his force. Nevertheless, the Navy Department instructed Rodgers to keep the British commander in chief of the coast of Ireland, Adm. Sir Lewis Bayly, informed of his movements and plans.[4] Likewise, the Admiralty instructed Bayly to keep Rodgers informed of the situation in his command.[5]

Bayly was notorious in the Royal Navy for being a singularly difficult man to deal with. Contrary to all expectations, though, he became a close friend of Admiral Sims and developed a warm relationship with the officers of the U.S. destroyer divisions serving at Queenstown, whom he referred to as "my Americans."[6] Just prior to the arrival of Division Six, Sims wrote to Bayly and included a copy of his instructions to Rodgers.

He apologetically explained that they were based on the Navy Department's plan and that he hoped to have that plan amended.[7]

Until the Navy Department and the Admiralty could agree on a joint plan, Division Six would operate according to the Navy Department's plan. Under this plan, Division Six would stand by at Berehaven, prepared to steam at four hours' notice. Upon receipt of a raider warning, the division would proceed to the Azores to protect shipping there and would escort eastbound convoys en route. Two divisions of U.S. destroyers from Queenstown were to join the battleships to furnish their screen.[8]

Withdrawing two divisions of destroyers from Queenstown, however, would disrupt the convoy system. Bayly explained to Rodgers that it was unlikely that more than six destroyers could join the battleships. He would have to withdraw these six destroyers from convoys that were west of St. George's Channel or the Scilly Islands. He could not reduce the escort of the troop convoys, nor reduce the whole escort of a cargo convoy, if the escort consisted entirely of U.S. destroyers. Nevertheless, Bayly promised to make every endeavor to send six destroyers as soon after a raider warning as possible.[9]

Rodgers decided to visit Bayly at Queenstown to discuss the matter of Division Six's destroyer screen. The British admiral held firm to his conviction that he could not release two full destroyer divisions as called for in the Navy Department's plan. Rodgers reported that Bayly would have to withdraw the six destroyers from sea duty and these would have to refuel before joining Division Six, which could cause a delay of up to twelve hours. Both admirals agreed that the battleships could not go to sea without them, however. Although Bayly refused to reduce further the destroyer escorts of the convoys, he was conciliatory about other issues. He agreed to petition the Admiralty for a gate in the eastern submarine net at Bantry Bay and he offered to provide all of the local transportation for the upcoming visit of Admiral Mayo and his staff.[10]

At 1805 on 10 September, Mayo and seven officers of his staff arrived at Berehaven after a very stormy crossing as passengers aboard the *Utah*, which was under the command of Capt. F. B. Bassett. Rodgers transferred his flag back to the *Utah* a few days later.[11]

Rodgers sympathized with Bayly's reluctance to reduce the already hard-pressed destroyer escort for the cargo convoys. He wrote to Sims and suggested that, in the new plan of operations, during a battle cruiser raid the destroyers should only escort the battleship division through the submarine zone and then resume their regular duties. When the battleships returned from the open Atlantic, they could radio the destroyers to escort them back to base. Rodgers revealed his opinion of the Navy Department's plan: "It appears to me that the destroyers would thus be better employed than in chasing around the ocean and running out of fuel."[12] Sims replied that, in using the destroyer escort, "You may exercise your discretion, adjusting your decision to circumstances as they present themselves at the time."[13] Sims was giving Rodgers permission to release his destroyer escort if he saw fit. It is not clear whether Sims had the Navy Department's approval in allowing Rodgers such wide discretion.

The shortage of destroyers hampered training exercises for the battleships. In order for the battleship division to hold gunnery exercises, destroyers from Queenstown were needed to provide a screen for them while practicing in Bantry Bay. Bayly agreed to detail destroyers for this purpose whenever they were available. On these occasions, Bayly would inform Rodgers two-and-a-half hours in advance of their arrival. The senior British naval officer at Berehaven would then quickly provide a target towing ship, and once the targets were in place, the division would carry out every drill possible: both independent and concentrated full-caliber firings, torpedo-defense firing, rangefinding and fire control exercises, paravane exercises, and the training of spotters. The division had to derive the maximum benefit from the limited time the destroyers were available.[14]

In a letter to Sims, Rodgers reported that Bayly had recently visited his flagship and that Bayly and his staff "have cordially helped with everything I have asked for." Rodgers did, however, complain again about the lack of a suitable escort for his division. Without the opportunity to venture outside of the anchorage for target practices, the efficiency of his division would suffer. Nevertheless, Rodgers promised to do his best with whatever he could get. He realized that there simply were not enough destroyers available.[15]

Sims replied that someday he hoped to have enough escorts based at Queenstown to give Division Six sufficient destroyers for conducting adequate exercises, but the shortage was so acute that any new destroyers from the United States were needed in other areas. The troop transports, for example, did not yet have sufficient escorts. Sims promised to do the best he could for Rodgers's division.[16]

In late September, Bayly found it possible to release four destroyers to Division Six for three days of sub-caliber practice. This would be the first target practice the division had carried out since coming to Berehaven. The *Utah* and *Oklahoma* had good sub-caliber practices and paravane drills, but the *Nevada* missed that opportunity because the minesweepers had to withdraw prematurely to Queenstown.[17]

About this same time, Division Six began using kite balloons for gunnery spotting.[18] During the following weeks, the new kite balloons suffered several disasters. In the early morning hours of 4 October, *Utah*'s kite balloon caught fire and was destroyed. Heavy rain was falling when the balloon caught fire. No one observed lightning, but it must have been the cause.[19] While at sea during the night of 14 October, lightning struck *Utah*'s replacement balloon, damaging it as well. That same night, high winds ripped *Oklahoma*'s balloon, and it fell to the sea and was not recovered. Fortunately, no observers died in any of these incidents, but from this point on, Division Six did not use observers in kite balloons during electrical storms.[20]

*

On 10 October, the Admiralty and the Navy Department finally agreed on Plan BCR, the joint plan to protect the troop convoys from German raiders. Only days later, they had to put the new plan into operation. On Monday, 14 October, at 0325, Rodgers received word that German cruisers might have escaped into the Atlantic.[21] If so, two troop convoys, HX 51 and HC 20, were in harm's way.

At 0440, Rodgers ordered the division to be ready for sea at one hour's notice. Fifteen minutes later, Bayly sent a dispatch informing Rodgers that the U.S. destroyers *Conyngham, Terry, Stevens, Downes, Samson, Allen,* and *Beale* would arrive at Berehaven at intervals between 0730 and 1630 to escort Division Six.[22] Rodgers immediately prepared to fuel the short-legged destroyers.

At 1756, Division Six and its screen got under way to rendezvous with the troop convoys. Owing to the heavy seas, the speed of the division was no higher than 15 knots. It was later that night that the storm destroyed first the *Utah*'s and then the *Oklahoma*'s kite balloons.

The next morning, 15 October, the destroyers began scouting for convoy HX 51. At 1030, the *Allen* reported a contact eight miles ahead. Twenty minutes later, the division sighted the convoy, twenty-two degrees on the port bow, eight miles distant. The battleships took station astern of the convoy in line abreast, at a distance of 600 yards. By 1700, the convoy was clear of the danger zone, and Division Six left them in the care of the destroyers and proceeded to meet convoy HC 20.

In the morning, Division Six had reached the approximate convoy position, but could not immediately locate it in visibility of only one to three miles. The battleships formed a scouting line, three miles apart, and started searching on an easterly course. At 0955, *Utah* finally spotted the convoy. The division reassembled without difficulty, and at 1712, U.S. destroyers from Queenstown, including the *Cassin, McCall, Balch, Paulding,* and *Kimberly,* joined the battleships to escort them back to Berehaven.[23] Division Six left their charges at 1800 on 16 October and anchored at Berehaven at 2345.[24]

The operation was a success, but the convoys were never actually in danger. This was to be the only time Division Six ever sortied to protect the troop convoys. No German raiders appeared, then or ever. The German Admiralty never ordered a battle cruiser raid against the troop convoys.[25] Nevertheless, the battleships remained ready for the possibility.

✳

At the end of October, Division Six had a new enemy to guard against. The epidemic of influenza began to spread in the cramped ships at an alarming rate. During the week ending 26 October, seven men from the *Nevada* died, along with another four from the *Utah* and four from the *Oklahoma.*[26] The division established a hospital with twenty-five beds at a nearby air station, along with an embalming station. Strict quarantine and liberal admission to the sick list kept the epidemic from spreading out of control. By 10 November, the day before the armistice, Rodgers reported that health conditions had improved dramatically and there were so few new cases of influenza that he considered that the epidemic was over. During that week, only two men from *Nevada* had died. During the epidemic, Division Six limited its drills to fire control and distribution exercises held at anchor, but on a regular basis.[27]

After the armistice, the *Arizona*, under Capt. John Drayton, left Hampton Roads on 18 November to join Division Six at Berehaven. That same day, the *Nevada* left Division Six to join Division Nine at 1550, replacing the *Florida*, which was returning to the United States. Accompanied by the destroyers *Stockton*, *McCall*, *Davis*, and *Trippe*, the *Nevada* arrived at Rosyth, the Grand Fleet base, on 23 November, too late to view the dramatic surrender of the German fleet.

Meanwhile, the *Utah* and *Oklahoma* moved to Portsmouth with an escort of four destroyers, the *Duncan*, *Terry*, *Downes*, and *Sterett*, in order to send the men on leave. British authorities arranged rail transport to London for the large leave parties from Division Six. At sea, the *Arizona* received a radio message to meet Division Six at Portsmouth rather than Berehaven. The *Arizona* arrived at Portsmouth at 1258 on 30 November. Just before midnight on 4 December, Division Nine and the *Nevada* joined Division Six at Portsmouth, uniting all of the U.S. battleships then in European waters.

During the closing months of the war, the Navy Department had promoted several of the battleship captains to the rank of rear admiral and transferred them to new posts.[28] In Division Nine, Capt. H. H. Christy had taken command of the *Wyoming*, Capt. E. L. Beach, the *New York*, Capt. L. R. Desteiger, the *Arkansas*, and Capt. M. M. Taylor, the *Florida*.[29] The new captains of Division Six were Capt. W. C. Cole of the *Nevada* and Capt. C. B. McVay of the *Oklahoma*.[30]

On Wednesday evening, 11 December, Sims arrived in Portsmouth, England, and assumed command of Divisions Six and Nine, raising his flag on the *Wyoming*. The battleships fueled and made preparations to leave Portsmouth to serve as President Wilson's escort to Brest, France. The next day, 40 officers and 425 men embarked as passengers, along with 40 newspaper reporters covering the president's journey. The U.S. battleships stood out from Portsmouth at 1100.

At 0730 on 13 December, they sighted the president's transport, the *George Washington*, in company with the battleship *Pennsylvania*, flagship of Adm. Henry Mayo, commander in chief of the Atlantic Fleet, and five destroyers. With flags flying from their mastheads, each ship of Divisions Six and Nine fired the national salute of twenty-one guns as the

George Washington passed their beam. Later that day, the president and his escort arrived at Brest. At about 1500, Wilson hauled down his flag from the *George Washington*. As he left on his historic mission to negotiate peace, the U.S. battleships again rendered the national salute to honor the president. Having accomplished their final mission of the war, the battleships left for the United States.[31]

Because no German surface raiders sortied against the troop convoys, the work of Battleship Division Six at Berehaven rarely appears as even a footnote in naval histories. There was no drama of battle on the high seas, but their task was significant nonetheless. A German battle cruiser raid against the convoys, even if not a high probability, was certainly a possibility that the Allies had to take seriously. Acting on the principle that prevention is better than remedy, the naval leadership acted to preempt and deter a German raid. Battleship Division Six never met the Germans in battle, but it did help to insure the safety of the valuable convoys. In this way, Division Six made its contribution to victory.

7

THE TWILIGHT OF THE GREAT WHITE FLEET

The Operations of U.S. Pre-Dreadnought
Battleships during World War I

❋

In a report on naval matters to President Woodrow Wilson in July 1917, journalist Winston Churchill first suggested using pre-dreadnought battleships to escort American troop convoys. At that time, the Navy Department considered such a use of capital ships as a heresy against the doctrine of fleet concentration. Only a year later, however, the exigencies of the naval war caused the naval leadership to disregard completely Alfred Thayer Mahan's warnings against any division of the fleet. At that point, the U-boat campaign no longer threatened to force Britain to sue for peace, and consequently the Navy Department no longer had to consider the possibility that the U.S. fleet might have to engage the High Seas Fleet alone. The combined U.S. and British fleets gave the Allies a large enough capital ship superiority over the Germans that they could safely detach major units for purposes other than a general fleet engagement. The new situation made it not only excusable, but expedient, for the Allies to use some of their surplus battleships to forestall Germany from using her capital ships in a guerre de course strategy.

❋

It is ironic that America's newest and most powerful battleships never entered the war zone before the armistice, while several of the obsolete pre-dreadnoughts did serve in European waters. The two modern *Pennsylvania*-class ships, launched in 1915, entered the war zone just after the armistice, and the two existing *New Mexico*–class ships never left U.S. waters. The *Pennsylvania* class was essentially an enlarged *Nevada* class with four triple turrets rather than two twin and two triple turrets.

The *New Mexico* class duplicated the *Pennsylvania* class, but introduced the 14-inch/50 caliber gun.[1]

The United States had twenty-three pre-dreadnought battleships at the outbreak of World War I. These ships were the legacy of the Spanish-American War, which had given a significant boost to naval construction, and the later the support of President Theodore Roosevelt, who saw a strong navy as the capstone of American commercial expansion and influence in international affairs. It was these pre-dreadnoughts that had comprised the Great White Fleet on its world cruise in 1907–9. The cruise of the Great White Fleet helped the United States to gain recognition as a world power, but as a battle fleet it was already obsolete. Britain's *Dreadnought*, completed in December 1906, made all previous battleships second-class. By eliminating all intermediate calibers, the all-big-gun ship had more than twice the firepower of any other battleship.[2]

The oldest U.S. pre-dreadnoughts were the three ships of the *Indiana* class—*Indiana, Massachusetts,* and *Oregon*—which were America's first modern battleships. Commissioned in 1893, the *Indiana* and *Oregon* participated in the Battle of Santiago during the Spanish-American War. They were not very successful because of the limited displacement and very low freeboard that characterized U.S. capital ships of the period. Besides their main armament, four 13-inch/35 caliber guns, they carried a mixed battery of eight 8-inch/35 caliber, four 6-inch/40 caliber, twenty 6-pounder, and six 1-pounder guns. The *Indiana*'s top speed was only 15 knots.

The *Iowa*, commissioned in 1893, was an improvement over the *Indiana* class because she had hydraulically trained turrets and a top speed of just over 17 knots. The *Kearsarge* and *Kentucky*, both completed in 1900, were easy to recognize because of their 8-inch turrets superimposed on the roofs of the 13-inch turrets. The over-and-under turrets trained together as a unit—an unfortunate arrangement because fire could not be divided between the two.

Launched in 1898, the year of the Spanish-American War, the three ships of the *Illinois* class had the same dimensions as the *Kearsarge* class, but differed greatly. The *Illinois*-class ships were the only U.S. battleships ever to have two funnels abreast.

The three ships of the *Maine* class were launched in 1901. These ships introduced the high-velocity 12-inch/40 caliber gun and were the first U.S. battleships to achieve 18 knots. An accidental explosion in the *Missouri*'s after turret in 1904 revealed deficiencies in U.S. turret design that were corrected in future designs.

During Theodore Roosevelt's presidency, 1901–9, four new battleship classes were laid down: the *Virginia, Connecticut, Vermont,* and *Mississippi* classes, totaling thirteen battleships. The Spanish-American War had settled the issue of whether the United States would have a coastal defense or a blue-water navy. The battleships built after 1898 had higher freeboard and greater displacements than their predecessors and could average 18 knots. The *Virginia* class reintroduced the superimposed turret, which the *Kearsarge* class had tested earlier, and which proved no more acceptable the second time around. The *Virginia*-class ships were, however, the fastest of the U.S. pre-dreadnoughts.

The *Connecticut* and *Vermont* classes, which differed mainly in armoring details, were an improvement over all previous designs. They were good sea boats and introduced a new rapid-fire 7-inch gun. They were the peak of U.S. pre-dreadnought design. The last class of pre-dreadnoughts, the *Mississippi* class, was a step backward. In an attempt to contain the growth of battleship size and cost, Congress limited them to a displacement of 13,000 tons. The main sacrifice was speed, for both ships of the class could attain only 17 knots. Completed in 1909, the Navy Department placed them in reserve as early as 1912, and sold them to Greece two years later. *Mississippi* and *Idaho,* renamed *Lemnos* and *Kilkis,* ended their long lives when German dive bombers sank both of them in Salamis harbor in 1941. Unfortunately, all thirteen of the battleships built during Roosevelt's tenure became obsolete within months of their completion because of the advent of the *Dreadnought.*[3]

At the beginning of the war, all but a few of the *Virginia-* and *Connecticut*-class pre-dreadnoughts were in reserve, but the Navy Department soon reactivated them. At that time, the Atlantic Fleet was divided into two parts: Force One, which included most of the pre-dreadnoughts; and Force Two, comprising the dreadnoughts and a slow division consisting of *South Carolina* and *Michigan*—America's first all-big-gun ships—and the pre-dreadnoughts *Vermont* and *Connecticut.* The *South Carolina* class was included in the slow division because they were restricted to 16,000 tons and, like the two pre-dreadnoughts, could

achieve only 18 knots. Consequently, they were not fast enough to operate tactically with the later dreadnoughts.[4]

✳

Throughout the war, the Atlantic Fleet worked to prepare itself for bat-
tle. It conducted constant divisional gunnery drills in the Chesapeake
Bay and regular fleet maneuvers at sea. The Atlantic Fleet base was at
Hampton Roads, Virginia, although a few times the fleet transferred to
Port Jefferson, in New York on Long Island Sound, for exercises. Force
One always accompanied the rest of the Atlantic Fleet for tactical exer-
cises at sea and had the same primary mission—to prepare for war.

During most of 1917, however, the pre-dreadnoughts of Force One
had the secondary role of training personnel for other ships in the fleet,
especially men for the engineering force and every rate of petty officer.
The shortage of experienced officers and men remained a problem for
the Atlantic Fleet for the duration of the war. Training programs could
not keep pace with the massive wartime expansion of the navy. Even the
dreadnoughts did not have full complements. Aside from training men
for the turret and handling crews for the new battleships *New Mexico*
and *Idaho*, the battleships of Force Two only had the capacity to prepare
their existing crews for battle. Therefore, the burden of training battleship recruits fell to Force One.[5]

The transfer of Battleship Division Nine to Berehaven, Ireland, in November 1917 placed new demands on the supply of trained men and led
to a revision of Force One's standing orders. Division Nine required full
complements before they joined the Grand Fleet, making the shortage
of trained men in the rest of the Atlantic Fleet even more severe. Consequently, the Navy Department made the training of officers and men
for other ships Force One's primary and immediate mission. In effect,
the pre-dreadnoughts became training ships with only a small nucleus of
permanently assigned officers and men. The officer trainees sent to the
pre-dreadnoughts were recent graduates of accelerated training programs at the Naval Academy in Annapolis and at the Naval Districts.
Many of the enlisted recruits were from the interior of the country and
had never been to sea before.[6]

Battleship Force One was under the command of Vice Adm. A. W.

Grant. Squadron One, comprising three divisions, was under the command of Rear Adm. Thomas Snowden. Officers of the National Naval Volunteer Reserve commanded the oldest ships of Squadron One.[7] Squadron One had the primary duty of training the engineer force.

Squadron Two trained the deck force and armed guard crews for merchant ships. The guard crews would man naval guns mounted on merchant ships to protect them from surfaced U-boats. These guns were usually 6-inch and 7-inch, removed from the secondary batteries of the battleships. Each gun crew included eight sailors and a leading petty officer, with two crews to a ship. After four weeks of practice with Squadron Two, the armed guards would carry out target practice while under way. If successful, they would transfer to the merchant ships. During the summer of 1918, the primary mission of Squadron Two shifted to training midshipmen, usually 175 midshipmen per ship. In addition, the entire force trained officers of the Naval Reserve.[8]

The practice of assigning extra recruits to the pre-dreadnoughts led to appallingly overcrowded conditions. While at sea, a bluejacket's life aboard the pre-dreadnoughts was miserable, and possibly no better than during the days of sail. Following a week's cruise during the summer of 1917, the executive officer of the Georgia, John Wainwright, reported on the deplorable conditions below decks: "When inspecting the gun deck on the night of recent moderately rough weather, the conditions were deplorable; men were packed in; the decks were running with water; and each man who had no swing was coiled down in any available corner." The Georgia was designed to billet 750 men, but had a complement of 1,045. Therefore, 325 men had no place to sleep, though this may not have been the worst privation. Wainwright reported, "The congestion in the head containing but thirty-six seats for this number of men can be realized; and having to be battened down forward, the unavoidable odor in spite of ample flushing was most obnoxious and sickening." He concluded that "ships are not made to float or fight under such conditions."[9]

The commander of the Georgia, Capt. S. E. Kittelle, forwarded the concerns of his executive officer, adding that the surgeons were convinced that the overcrowded conditions would become a hazard to the health of the crew if there was extensive cruising in bad weather. In spite of the poor conditions, however, Kittelle reported that the crew was on the whole the most cheerful he had ever commanded.

Kittelle's report pointed out several serious personnel deficiencies, which posed problems for the rest of the force as well. There were so few experienced watch officers that heads of departments had to stand watch because they were the only officers who were competent enough. Kittelle stated that, although he understood the need to train officers of the national volunteer reserve, "their progress in ship handling, is with one exception only, discouragingly slow." Furthermore, he complained that the Navy Department's rapid expansion was resulting in the enlistment of below average recruits. In his opinion, most of the enlisted men of the deck force were too young and immature, and the number of them who would be capable of eventually becoming petty officers was quite low. Kittelle expressed his belief that the recruits would develop more rapidly if they were scattered over a number of ships with experienced men, instead of being placed in large groups together.[10]

In his report to Adm. Henry Mayo, commander in chief of the Atlantic Fleet, regarding this same summer 1917 cruise, Admiral Grant observed, "The cruise was most beneficial in demonstrating the inexperience of the personnel." Gun pointers thought to be ready for target practice still needed additional training. The youth and inexperience of the crews detracted from the efficiency of ship drills and engineering performances. Grant reported that aboard the *Virginia*, 87 percent of the crew had never been to sea before. More serious, most of the officers themselves still needed elementary instruction. Commanders had to rely on these same inexperienced officers to train the inexperienced crews— a case of the blind leading the blind.[11]

From 14 to 18 January 1918, Force One exercised at sea with the battle fleet. The fleet endured heavy squalls on the morning of 15 January and suffered a series of accidents. At about 1045, both the *Texas* and *North Dakota* signaled they had men overboard. Each vessel had lost three men. After dropping out of cruising formation, each managed to rescue one of its men. A fifth man was killed when a falling hatch hit him in the head. At 1335, *Michigan* lost her entire foremast. The ship had rolled heavily to port and then lurched suddenly to starboard, snapping the cage mast at the narrowest point of its hour-glass shape, near the spot where a fragment of an exploding 12-inch gun had torn through the mast in 1916. The searchlights, directorscope, and the heavy fire control tops were a mass of debris on the boat deck. The collapse of the mast killed six men and injured thirteen, three of them seriously. Altogether, the fleet lost eleven men during the exercise. Grant believed that the loss of men overboard was due to their inexperience and lack of respect for heavy seas. He commented that the cruise was good experience for the men, and "particularly beneficial in teaching them what to expect of a storm."[12]

On 1 June 1918, Force One had a serious gunnery accident that showed the state of gunnery training in the force left much to be desired. The *New Hampshire* and *Louisiana* were to hold daylight torpedo-defense practice on Chesapeake Bay, and the ships had been at anchor since 0500 waiting for a dense fog to clear. The fog lifted enough to begin the practice by 0900. The *Ohio* was acting as the towing vessel. Two submarine chasers positioned themselves off her bow, port and starboard. The *Louisiana*, waiting her turn to fire, was about five hundred yards astern. The *New Hampshire* began the second leg of her run, firing the forward starboard battery of three 7-inch guns at a range of between five and six thousand yards. Two of the guns began firing on the port submarine chaser. In an attempt to stop the *New Hampshire* from firing on the submarine chaser, the *Ohio* signaled "Cease Fire" by siren, steam whistle, searchlights, signal flags, and radio—all without success until after *New Hampshire* had fired six to eight salvos.

Meanwhile, the submarine chaser zigzagged toward the *Louisiana* in an attempt to escape the firing. Observing the fall of shot and realizing what was happening, the commander of the *Louisiana* sounded general quarters to get his men behind armor. Most of the shells landed near the submarine chaser, but as the smaller craft neared the *Louisiana*, one of the *New Hampshire*'s shells struck the bow of the *Louisiana*. The projectile passed through the chief petty officers' compartment and the sick bay before passing out the starboard side of the ship. Fragments killed one man and injured several others in the sick bay.[13]

The incompetence did not end with the accident, for after the shell struck the *Louisiana*, all three battleships went dead in the water. By stopping, the ships were putting themselves at risk; earlier in the war, U-9 had been able to sink the British cruisers *Aboukir, Cressy,* and *Hogue* when two of the ships stopped to render aid to the other. At 1100, two observers aboard the *Ohio* spotted a disturbance in the water and reported a periscope 1,200 yards away. Shortly thereafter, two men on the bridge of the *Louisiana* also reported spotting a periscope. The three battleships got under way and the *New Hampshire* and *Ohio* opened fire on the wake, firing around twenty-one 6-inch shells. The submarine chasers investigated but did not discover anything.[14]

Following the damage to the *Louisiana* and the poor results of a recent battle inspection, Grant wrote a report that was highly critical of the practice of relying heavily upon officers of the naval reserve and naval volunteers. Referring to Squadron One's naval volunteer officers, Grant wrote:

> In view of the length in commission of these vessels, it is considered that the feature of commissioning vessels entirely with volunteer officers has been a very thorough trial. The results demonstrate its complete failure. The ships are of value neither as training units nor for military operations of any description. In view of this feature, they constitute an element of military weakness and the experiment should not be repeated. The fault lay not with the zeal or with the intelligence of the personnel, but with their lack of experience and a general lack of knowledge both of the military standards and of what must be accomplished with a man-of-war.[15]

At least indirectly, these views were an indictment of the administration's policy of mobilization and rapid expansion after the U.S. entry into the war. Grant's criticism of his reserve officers was equally severe:

> Even in the case of officers who have been in the service a considerable length of time, having entered as officers without previous experience in the fundamentals of discipline or in the duties which are primarily required of a division officer, they are naturally unable as a class to train the recruits in those matters that fall peculiarly within their province. The practice of commissioning such officers before they have passed through and personally performed the duties which they must as division officers teach others to perform is believed to be faulty, and it is believed that they should be promoted to officers only after passing through a very thorough and strict course as reserve midshipmen.[16]

Grant was also critical of the material condition of his battleships. In another report following the battle inspection of 30 June, he emphasized the large amount of repair and alteration work the ships needed. The strain of operating under war conditions revealed the poor condition of the ships and their need for alterations. Grant pointed out that many of these problems had been apparent before the war, but because they were not essential for cruising efficiency, the Navy Department had not made the necessary alterations. At least regarding the pre-dreadnought fleet, the Navy had a peacetime standard that was far below the wartime standard of efficiency. Grant suggested that in the future there should be regular periods during peace when the fleet operated under war conditions to reveal and correct defects before an emergency. He ended his report with a warning: "In the present war, we have been fortunate in the ability to make these alterations without molestation by the enemy. Such conditions may not exist in future wars."[17]

The most important alteration, or repair, that the ships needed was to restore the structural integrity of the watertight bulkheads. Since the ships' construction, most of the bulkheads had been pierced for electrical conduits, speaking tubes, and water or steam piping. Because of higher-priority work, the naval yards could not undertake major overhauls of the pre-dreadnoughts, so Grant organized work parties from the ships' crews to plug holes, shore up bulkheads, and subject every watertight bulkhead to an air-pressure test.[18]

On 29 September 1918, the Minnesota left Hampton Roads with the destroyer Israel as escort, headed for the Philadelphia Navy Yard. At 0318, twenty miles from Fenwick Island, she hit a mine. The explosion obliterated the hull structure between frames 5 and 16 and from the keel to the lower edge of the armor belt. The forward compartments flooded, but the newly repaired watertight bulkheads held. Grant believed that these repairs saved the Minnesota. He doubted that any of the pre-dreadnoughts could have survived such an underwater explosion before the bulkheads had been repaired.

At ten knots, the Minnesota managed to limp into Delaware Bay, arriving at the Philadelphia Navy Yard at 0748. U-117, cruising southward off the coast of Maryland, was probably responsible for laying the mine. Minnesota was fortunate to have survived the mine. The damage was so extensive that she was out of commission until February 1919.[19]

*

In late July 1918, as described earlier, the Navy Department made plans to begin using pre-dreadnoughts as escorts for U.S. troop convoys. In late August, the Navy Department extended the plan to include using pre-dreadnought escorts to protect the mixed troop and mercantile convoys from New York and Halifax. From September 1918 until the end of the war, the pre-dreadnoughts and *South Carolina*-class dreadnoughts of Force One served as escorts for the U.S. troop convoys and the mixed mercantile and troop convoys from New York.

These convoys were the responsibility of the Cruiser and Transport Force of the Atlantic Fleet, under the command of Rear Adm. Albert Gleaves. The cruiser force, which included all of the U.S. cruisers and armored cruisers, would be an adequate defense against the average commerce raider, but would be no match for a battle cruiser. Only the addition of a battleship could protect the convoys against an attack by a German battle cruiser. Whenever one of the ships of Force One was escorting a convoy, it came under the operational control of Admiral Gleaves.[20]

The British were willing to provide some of their own pre-dreadnoughts of the *King Edward VII* class to escort Atlantic convoys, but they did not have enough trained personnel to man them. In October the Navy Department offered to man the British pre-dreadnoughts in order to start them escorting the convoys. The British agreed to this scheme, but first had to overhaul the ships before they would be ready for service. The war would end before the *King Edward VII*–class ships were ready for escort duty, and only U.S. pre-dreadnoughts ultimately served as escorts for the transatlantic convoys.[21]

The *South Carolina, New Hampshire,* and *Kansas* became the first battleships to escort a convoy across the Atlantic on 6 September 1918. This convoy was one of the HX, or fast mercantile and troop convoys from New York. The HX convoys were designated as "fast" because they maintained a speed of 13 knots, which was faster than that of other merchant convoys. The journey across was uneventful. The battleships parted company with the convoy when their coal bunkers were nearly half empty on 16 September.

The return trip was more difficult than the journey into the war zone. The day after leaving the convoy, the *South Carolina* lost her starboard propeller. She continued, using only the port engine, at 11 knots. Then at

1630 on 20 September the port engine suddenly stopped. A throttle valve had malfunctioned. The ship got under way again using an auxiliary throttle, but the new arrangement caused severe vibration. At 2230 the ship stopped again and remained motionless for six hours while the main valve was repaired. The battleships finally reached U.S. waters on 24 September and *South Carolina* limped on to the Philadelphia Naval Yard for repairs.[22]

Nebraska escorted the next convoy across the Atlantic. On 17 September she left New York as the heavy escort for the fast merchant convoy HX 49. Also part of the escort were the armed merchant cruiser *Rochester*, the destroyer *Dent*, and the British armed merchant cruiser *Arlanza*. The *Arlanza* was the regular escort for that particular convoy, and her commander was in charge of handling the convoy, which included ten British merchantmen and the tanker *Cuyama* of the Naval Overseas Transportation Service.[23]

Again, the journey across the Atlantic was uneventful. The *Nebraska* escorted the convoy to an eastern rendezvous with the British escorts that would protect the convoy for the remainder of the voyage. She returned to Hampton Roads on 3 October.[24]

The *Georgia* escorted U.S. troop convoy group 67, which left New York on 23 September. The convoy included nine troop transports, with the armored cruisers *North Carolina* and *Montana* and the destroyer *Rathburne* as the rest of the escort. The weather during the eastward run was very heavy, and the convoy had to slow to 10 knots because some of the transports could not maintain their cruising speed. As a consequence, the convoy was twelve hours late in arriving at the eastern rendezvous.

Because the *Georgia* had taken on 526 tons of coal more than her bunker capacity, she handled poorly and pitched heavily during the transit. The gun deck was even wetter than usual, and because the ship was battened down, it was poorly ventilated as well. Combined with the overcrowding, conditions were ripe for the spread of disease. The *Georgia* had 120 cases of influenza, 14 cases of pneumonia, and 7 deaths during the trip. In spite of the extra coal, the *Georgia* did not have sufficient fuel to accompany the convoy all the way to the rendezvous point. She had to return to base before delivering the convoy to the eastern escort force. The *North Carolina*, however, had enough range to remain with the convoy until the rendezvous with the destroyers from Britain. In his report, Captain Kittelle suggested that the installation of a new type of turbo-generator would increase the steaming efficiency enough to extend the range.[25]

The next important convoy to sail from New York, HX 50, left on 25 September. Convoy HX 50 was a mercantile convoy of eight British ships bound for Liverpool and three more en route to Glasgow. This convoy had a large escort force, including the *Louisiana*, the armored cruiser *St. Louis*, and the British merchant cruiser *Otranto*. Antisubmarine craft in company included two destroyers and six submarine chasers. The convoy also had air cover. Three balloons, the *Xarifa, Bagley,* and *Gloucester,* along with a dirigible and three seaplanes, patrolled the skies above the convoy. The voyage was uneventful, and as usual for that time of year, the weather was bad. Near the Grand Banks, the fog was so thick that the *Louisiana* lost sight of the rest of the convoy for sixty hours.

On 4 October the convoy reached the rendezvous and the *Louisiana* began the trip back to Hampton Roads. Before leaving New York, the crew had built additional bunkers for extra coal on the gun deck in the casemates of some of the 7-inch guns. In spite of the extra supply, the expenditure of coal was greater than expected, and by 8 October it appeared that there would not be sufficient coal to reach Hampton Roads with any margin of safety. Therefore, the *Louisiana* stopped for coaling at Halifax before returning to base on 17 October.[26]

On 30 September the dreadnought *Michigan*, the armored cruiser *South Dakota*, and the destroyers *Bell* and *Fairfax* sailed with U.S. troop convoy group 70. The convoy included detachments from New York, Philadelphia, and Newport News. En route, the ships received a warning from the Navy Department that German raiders could have sortied into the Atlantic. The U.S. military attaché at Bern, Switzerland, had obtained information that two German cruisers had left Kiel on 29 September for a raid against the U.S. troop convoys. However, the Germans had not sortied; the intelligence from the military attaché was nothing more than a rumor.

The convoy arrived in European waters unmolested, but without the *Michigan*. On 8 October she lost her port propeller and had to leave the convoy well before reaching the eastern rendezvous. She returned to base safely at 11 knots. It is curious that both the *Michigan* and her sister ship lost propellers within weeks of one another.[27]

The pre-dreadnoughts escorted three more convoys during the month of October. The *Nebraska* left New York on 13 October as escort to mercantile convoy HX 52, twelve British ships bound for Liverpool. The armored cruiser *Montana* and the British armed merchant cruiser *Edinburgh Castle* also served as escorts.[28] The *Kansas*, the U.S. armed merchant cruiser *Rochester*, the British armed merchant cruiser *Andes*, and the destroyer *Dent* furnished the escort for the next fast merchant convoy from New York, HX 53.[29] The *Louisiana* then escorted troop convoy group 78, consisting of ten U.S. troop ships and two cargo ships. This convoy sailed directly to Brest, France.[30]

During November, the last month of the war, the pre-dreadnoughts escorted their three final convoys. The *Georgia* was the principal escort for U.S. troop convoy group 80. This convoy included four U.S. transports and the U.S. hospital ship *Mercy*.[31] The *Virginia* escorted U.S. troop convoy 83, which included five transports.[32] On 13 November the *Nebraska*, along with the U.S. destroyer *Talbot* and the British armed merchant cruiser *Teutonic*, escorted the last convoy from the United States to European waters. Convoy HX 56 included six British ships bound for Liverpool. The *Nebraska* returned from convoy duty on 2 December.

✷

The final duty of the pre-dreadnoughts was to provide transport for American troops returning from France. Cdr. C. S. Freeman, executive officer of the *South Carolina*, had first broached the idea of using battleships as troop transports *to* the war zone in a memorandum to Secretary Daniels on 28 January 1918. Freeman had pointed out that the pre-dreadnought battleships were militarily inactive except for training and that they could be making a more direct contribution:

> Nearly half a million tons of shipping, built for a military purpose, aging rapidly in a military sense and doomed to early obsolescence, is occupying a passive role in the greatest war of history. I submit simply that this tonnage should be put to some effective military use. . . . If our battleships cannot actively engage the enemy and are not needed to contain the enemy, it is essential, in order that their role may be an active one, that they bring pressure to bear upon the enemy by projecting man power within striking distance of the battle front.[33]

Freeman maintained that transport duty would actually accelerate the training of officers and men. The ships would have to trim their swollen complements, but the increased amount of time at sea would make up for the smaller crews. He conceded that the number of troops transported would be smaller than aboard properly fitted transports, probably around 1,000 soldiers per battleship. Nevertheless, every battalion transported in a battleship would release an equivalent amount of regular transport tonnage.[34]

Answering Freeman's memorandum on behalf of Daniels, Chief of Naval Operations Benson thanked him for his ideas but replied that the department did not wish to use the pre-dreadnoughts for transports at that time. Admiral Benson stated that three conditions would have to arise before it would be prudent to use battleships as troop carriers: no longer any need for offensive action, no necessity for supporting or protecting the lines of supply, and a need for troops and supplies so acute that regular transports could not meet the demands. The department believed that the small troop loads the pre-dreadnoughts could carry did not justify the large amount of fuel they would burn.[35]

Although the Navy Department had declined to use the pre-dreadnoughts for troop transports during the war, immediately after the armistice it began planning to use them to return the troops from abroad. Admiral Grant, acting commander in chief of the Atlantic Fleet while Admiral Mayo was abroad, submitted a report on 14 November detailing the numbers of army officers and men that the individual battleships of the fleet could transport. He recommended that if the department had to use battleships as transports, then they should employ only the pre-dreadnoughts and not first-line battleships. He pointed to the unsettled political conditions and the deterioration of efficiency that months of transport work would cause. Grant also advised against using the older pre-dreadnoughts—the *Indiana, Ohio,* and *Kearsarge* classes— given their limited range and restricted accommodations.[36]

The Navy Department's proposal to use the pre-dreadnoughts as transports sparked a clash between Benson and Mayo. When word of the department's plan reached Mayo, he voiced his opposition in a cable to Benson in Paris:

> I wish to strongly urge and earnestly protest against the use of battleships, cruisers, or destroyers for the transporting of troops. Such use would destroy

their military efficiency and put the fleet back a year or two just at a time when every effort should be made to maintain the fleet at the highest point of efficiency.

Mayo ended the cable by urging that the department take no action on the plan until he had a chance to see the secretary personally in December.[37]

Benson replied that while he did not mind Mayo discussing the matter with the secretary, he thought it inappropriate that Mayo wanted to deliver his protest to the secretary personally and not through the chief of naval operations:

> In my opinion it is highly improper for such matters to be presented to the secretary in person before they have been presented to me. In the spirit of fairness I have always made it a point to see that your views were thoroughly understood by the secretary. I think you will agree that it is necessary in a matter of this character for my final decision to hold.[38]

Benson's decision held. By 3 December the Navy Department had already sent movement orders to Battleship Force One for two pre-dreadnoughts to sail for Brest each week, beginning on 10 December.[39]

The first of these, *Georgia* and *Kansas*, arrived at Brest on 22 December after a twelve-day voyage. The time in port was four days. Together, they embarked 2,732 officers and men. The next relay, the *Virginia* and the *Rhode Island*, arrived in Brest on 30 December and took aboard 2,043 officers and men. Their time in port was three days. On 5 January 1919 the *Louisiana* and the *New Hampshire* arrived at Brest and embarked 2,169 officers and men, including eight civilians. Again, the time in port was only three days. Combined, these six pre-dreadnoughts transported 6,944 officers and men during the first month. In addition, the Navy Department was also operating the armored cruisers *North Carolina*, *Seattle*, *Huntington*, *St. Louis*, *Montana*, *South Dakota*, and *Pueblo* as troop transports. During the first month of transport duty, the pre-dreadnoughts and armored cruisers together carried a total of 17,272 officers and men home from abroad.[40]

At least two Army officers were impressed with their accommodations on the pre-dreadnoughts and had comfortable voyages. After the first transport trip of the *Georgia*, the senior Army officer among the passengers reported, "I consider this trip a more desirable and satisfactory one than that taken when going to France on a large ocean liner owned by another government." The officer was impressed with the good food, fresh air in the sleeping compartments, and good sanitation.[41] Maj. J. F. Dillon, after his journey aboard the *Nebraska*, sent the ship's captain a letter of thanks and commendation. Dillon reported that it was the unanimous opinion of his officers and men that "not a single act was overlooked on the part of the ship's personnel, that might add to our comfort, convenience or enjoyment of the journey." He added that the food was excellent and that relations between the Army and Navy enlisted men were "cordial and amicable."[42]

Compared to life in the trenches, the accommodations aboard a battleship must have seemed pleasant. The troops did, however, have to adjust to myriad rules and regulations that they probably were not used to. Troops boarding the *Minnesota* were issued a pamphlet detailing the rules of behavior aboard ship. The following were prohibited:

> Using obscene or profane language.
> Gambling.
> Leaning on life lines.
> Matches other than safety matches.
> Intoxicating liquor in possession.
> Obstructing passageways or ladders.
> Visiting between Army and Navy enlisted men.
> Sleeping on deck.
> Throwing anything over the side.
> Spitting on deck.
> Permitting water to stand in buckets.
> Clogging urinals and latrine troughs.
> Making noise after taps.
> Injuring government property.
> Opening any port or hatch found closed.
> Turning on or off electric lights or switches.
> Whistling.
> Going in any boat on boat deck.
> Going to head bare-footed and returning to hammock.

Running to mess tables.
Throwing food.
Smoking out of hours.
To sell, give away, or exchange Army or Navy clothing.
Bartering with Navy Personnel.

In addition, there were the usual admonitions against wasting fresh water, showing lights, and allowing litter in the living compartments. To help enforce the regulations, there was an Army police detail of 10 non-commissioned officers and 150 troops.[43]

Transport aboard the pre-dreadnoughts may have been satisfactory for the Army personnel, but transport duty did have adverse effects on the morale and efficiency of the Navy crews. The commander of the *Georgia* reported that transport duty had lowered the standard of appearance for the ship and produced a "lack of smartness in the appearance of the crew due to the fact that the men are kept constantly at work out at sea cleaning . . . and in port coaling ship." Likewise, the commanding officer of the *Virginia* complained, "Under present operating schedule time for overhaul, cleaning boilers, etc., is not sufficient to keep up with current needs."[44] The *Vermont*'s commander warned, "As far as the fighting efficiency of the personnel is concerned, all efficiency will soon disappear and at the end of about nine months of this duty any knowledge of gunnery or any skill that has been acquired will be nothing beyond a memory."[45] The pre-dreadnought captains clearly did not appreciate transport duty.

A disagreement over the number of passengers that the battleships could carry caused a conflict between the commander of Battleship Force One, Admiral Grant, and the commander of the Cruiser and Transport Force, Admiral Gleaves. The two admirals exercised a sort of dual command: while on transport duty the pre-dreadnoughts were under the command of Gleaves, but between trips they returned to the control of Grant. It was Grant's responsibility to provide recommendations to Gleaves regarding logistics, upkeep measures, and drills, while Gleaves was to furnish Grant with recommendations regarding matters affecting the usefulness of the vessels as transports. The two admirals had poorly defined jurisdictions over the pre-dreadnoughts because they were to consult each another about their policies.[46]

The trouble began after the *Kansas* made two voyages carrying 1,690 and 1,925 troops, respectively. This contravened Grant's orders not to exceed 1,200 men, which he believed was the maximum that could be shipped and still maintain watertight integrity and acceptable sanitary conditions. Grant was angered that the commander of the *Kansas*, Capt. B. F. Hutchinson, had ignored his orders, but Gleaves praised the officer for transporting more troops. Benson sent Grant a cable asking why the *Kansas* could haul so many troops but the other pre-dreadnoughts could not. He also wanted to know why Grant's battleships remained in U.S. ports for fourteen days between trips while Gleaves's cruisers needed only seven days in port. Benson ordered Grant to increase the troop-carrying capacity of his battleships.[47]

Grant responded by sending a lengthy memorandum to Benson explaining his policies, condemning the actions of Hutchinson, and complaining about Gleaves's lack of support. Grant justified limiting the number of troops by including a report from the commander of the *Pueblo*, one of Gleaves's cruisers. After a trip in which the *Pueblo* had carried 2,200 passengers, her commander reported that sanitary conditions had been very bad, and because of the need to keep hatches closed, the air below decks was very foul. He added that had a contagious disease appeared, it could have become an epidemic. Grant noted that *Kansas* had also had many additional cases of contagious disease because of the overcrowding. He reminded Benson that if an epidemic started among the troops, there would be a scandal.

Grant's criticism of Hutchinson was harsh and direct. In his opinion, the commanding officer of the *Kansas* had exceeded his instructions and shown poor professional judgment: "The Commander of Battleship Force One is of the opinion that the Commanding Officer of the *Kansas* is deserving of reprimand rather than of commendation in regard to this matter." Grant bitterly complained about Gleaves's implied criticism of the other pre-dreadnought captains for not transporting as many troops as *Kansas* did. He pointed out that those commanders were the ones who had obeyed orders and exercised good professional judgment.[48] Grant apparently made his point. The pre-dreadnoughts continued his policy of transporting only 1,200 troops.[49]

✳

After a conference with representatives of the War Department in June, the Navy Department decided that the pre-dreadnoughts would end their transport duty on or before 1 August 1919.[50] By July all of the U.S. troops had returned from France. The cruiser and transport force carried a total of 1,493,626 troops home from the war in 115 ships, including the pre-dreadnoughts and armored cruisers.[51]

After their transport duty, the pre-dreadnoughts underwent repairs at the Norfolk and Philadelphia navy yards. In October 1919, the *Nebraska*, under the command of Capt. P. N. Olmstead, joined the Pacific Fleet, but remained in service only one year. Throughout 1920 the Navy Department decommissioned most of the pre-dreadnoughts, which were either sold for scrap or sunk as targets between 1920 and 1924.[52]

A few of the old ships lingered on as noncombatant ships. The *Minnesota* remained in service as the training ship for the summer cruises of midshipmen from the Naval Academy until 1921; she was sold in 1924.[53] The *Oregon* became a floating memorial in 1925. In 1942, she was sold to the breakers, but the Navy had the work stopped, and used her as an ammunition hulk during the 1944 invasion of Guam. She remained at Guam until the Navy sold her after the war. The *Kearsarge* became a crane ship until the Navy scrapped her in 1955. The *Illinois* served first as an armory, and later as an accommodation ship from 1921 until 1955. Sadly, none of the pre-dreadnought battleships have survived as monuments to the period of history when the United States became a naval power.[54]

Most of the ships of the Great White Fleet lived very short lives. Built in the midst of a revolution of naval technology, they became obsolete soon after, or sometimes before, their launching. Little more than two decades after their construction, most were already on the scrap heap. In spite of their obsolescence, the pre-dreadnoughts of the Atlantic Fleet saw extensive service during World War I. Because the Allies had the luxury of superior numbers of capital ships, they could release their older battleships for duties other than preparing for battle with the High Seas Fleet. The work the pre-dreadnoughts performed—as training ships, escorts, and transports—was not glamorous. They nevertheless played a more active role in the war than the most modern battleships of the fleet.

CONCLUSION

*

The naval war evolved in unexpected ways. The mine and the torpedo restricted the movements of the rival battle fleets. The danger of minefields and submarine ambushes made a close-blockade impossible and turned the North Sea into a kind of "no-man's land" for capital ships. The Grand Fleet and the High Seas Fleet only ventured into those waters for specific operations and under favorable conditions.[1] The numerically inferior German fleet would accept battle only under specific circumstances: if they could isolate a part of the British fleet, if they could lead the British into a submarine trap to reduce their numbers, or if the British were foolhardy enough to enter the mine-infested waters of Heligoland Bight. Therefore, the chances of a decisive fleet engagement were slim.

As a result of the stalemate in the North Sea, the use of the blockade dominated the naval strategies of both protagonists. The British fleet isolated Germany from most of the outside world by controlling both the northern and southern approaches of the North Sea. Germany mounted a counter-blockade with her U-boats, threatening Britain's vital seaborne trade. Although the submarine campaign became the critical issue of the naval war, the opposing battle fleets were an integral, if indirect, part of submarine warfare. The High Seas Fleet was the power behind the U-boat campaign. If not for the High Seas Fleet, the Allies could have effectively mined the approaches to the German bases and prevented the egress of the U-boats. Likewise, the strength of the Grand Fleet was the real power behind the blockade of Germany and the war against the U-boats.

The U.S. Navy Department at first held to its traditional strategy of keeping the U.S. fleet concentrated to await the decisive battle with the enemy fleet, but, concentrated in U.S. waters, the Atlantic Fleet could not bring its power to bear directly against Germany. Nor was it necessary or expedient for the entire battle fleet to move to European waters. The Navy Department recognized the contradiction between its strategy and its wartime responsibilities and finally abandoned strict adherence to the principles of Mahan. Thereafter, individual units could and did make important and needed contributions.

The cooperation of Battleship Division Nine with the British Grand Fleet was a significant contribution to the war effort. The addition of the U.S. battleships gave the Grand Fleet an unqualified superiority in battleships over the German fleet. With the added battleship strength, the Grand Fleet could protect North Sea commerce and mining operations, while still maintaining the blockade.

The U.S. battleships played an active role in North Sea operations and became an integral part of the British Grand Fleet. This experience of joint operations with the British benefited the entire U.S. fleet by exposing ships and men to British methods and experience. In addition, service in the war zone was invaluable in revealing deficiencies that may not have otherwise come to light. The operational cooperation of the American squadron with the Grand Fleet was an unprecedented success. The two navies had never cooperated as allies before. Nevertheless, neither national pride nor conflicting strategic ideas or personalities interfered with the amalgamation of the American ships into the Grand Fleet.

Protecting the sea lanes between the United States and France was as important as supporting the blockade of Germany. The primary contribution of the U.S. Navy during the war was the transport of U.S. troops, along with their supplies, to the Western Front. There was the real possibility that Germany would use her capital ships to raid the transatlantic convoys, and the only way to ensure the safety of the troop convoys was to protect them with battleships. Again, the large capital ship superiority of the Allies allowed the diversion of surplus battleships from their traditional duty—engaging or preparing to engage the enemy fleet—to fulfill other needs.

The spectacle of battleships, even obsolete ones, shepherding individual convoys shows the extent that the role of the battleship changed during World War I. The need for battle fleets remained, but the war had ended rigid observance of Mahan's doctrine of fleet concentration. In the next war, the United States would wield a two-ocean navy. The nontraditional use of battleships would also repeat itself. Throughout World War II, the Royal Navy would use its battleships to escort important convoys, and the U.S. Navy would use its as carrier escorts and antiaircraft gun platforms. Both navies would further develop the use of battleships for fire support for amphibious landings.

The U.S. Navy worked under a serious handicap during World War I. Because the United States did not mobilize until after the declaration of war, training programs could not keep pace with the navy's rapid expansion. Many of the deficiencies of the U.S. battleships during the war can be traced to the shortage of trained officers and men. The poor gunnery of the American squadron when it joined the Grand Fleet and the friendly-fire incident between the *New Hampshire* and the *Louisiana* exhibit the poor state of training in the U.S. fleet during the war. The U.S. Navy would begin the Second World War with eleven times more officers and men than it had when it entered the First.[2]

U.S. battleship operations in World War I were not as glamorous as a decisive fleet engagement along classical lines, but they were important nonetheless. It should be remembered that the Allies won the war at sea without a decisive encounter between the rival fleets. The addition of the U.S. battleships allowed the Allies to protect the supply lines from the United States without withdrawing units from the North Sea and weakening the naval blockade of Germany. The influence of the U.S. battle fleet was indirect, but substantial.

NOTES

✳

Chapter 1 / The Exorcism of Mahan's Ghost

1. The Lansing-Ishii agreement pledged both powers to respect China's territorial integrity, but it acknowledged that Japan had "special interests" in China. The agreement temporarily improved relations between the United States and Japan.

2. Dean C. Allard, "Anglo-American Naval Differences during World War I," *Military Affairs* 44 (April 1980): 77.

3. David Trask, *Captains and Cabinets: Anglo-American Naval Relations, 1917–1918* (Columbia: University of Missouri Press, 1972), 55–60.

4. Josephus Daniels, *The Wilson Era: Years of War and After, 1917–1923* (Chapel Hill: University of North Carolina Press, 1946), 41–43, 67.

5. "Excerpt of Speech by Daniels," 11 December 1917, TD File, Subject File 1911–1927, Record Group 45, National Archives (this subject file hereafter cited as RG 45).

6. Mary Klachko and David Trask, *Admiral William Shepherd Benson: First Chief of Naval Operations* (Annapolis, Md.: Naval Institute Press, 1987), 57–58. Klachko points out that during a congressional investigating committee hearing in 1920, Admiral Benson admitted he had warned Sims against British machinations but wanted to counter the idea that he was anti-British.

7. Ibid., 63.

8. "Memorandum by Jellicoe," 9 April 1917, TP File, RG 45.

9. Browning to Admiralty, memorandum, 9 April 1917, in ADM 137/1436, Admiralty Records, Public Record Office.

10. Klachko and Trask, *William Shepherd Benson*, 65.

11. Alfred T. Mahan, *The Influence of Sea Power on History: 1660–1783*, 12th ed. (Boston: Little, Brown and Co., 1918).

12. William Livezey, *Mahan on Sea Power* (Norman: University of Oklahoma Press, 1986), 297–332.

13. Mahan, *Influence of Sea Power*, 6–9, 118, 199; and Peter Paret, ed., *Makers of Modern Strategy: From Machiavelli to the Nuclear Age* (Princeton University Press, 1986), 457–59.

14. Robert L. O'Connell, *Sacred Vessels: The Cult of the Battleship and the Rise of the U.S. Navy* (New York: Oxford University Press, 1991), 78–79.

15. The First Sea Lord is the British equivalent of the chief of naval operations in the U.S. Navy.

16. William S. Sims, *The Victory at Sea* (New York: Doubleday, Page, and Co., 1920), 5–9.

17. Sims to Navy Department, 14 April 1917, series 2 (microfilm), Papers of President Woodrow Wilson, Manuscript Division, Library of Congress, Washington, D.C.

18. Sims to Daniels, 18 April 1917, series 2 (microfilm), Papers of President Wilson.

19. Sims to Daniels, 19 April 1917, in Senate Committee on Naval Affairs, *Hearings before the Subcommittee of the Committee on Naval Affairs*, 66th Cong., 2d sess., 7 April 1920.

20. De Chair to Admiralty, "General Report on the Progress of Negotiations with the United States Navy Department, etc., in Connection with Mr. Balfour's Mission," 15 May 1917, ADM 137/1436, Admiralty Records.

21. David Lloyd George, *The War Memoirs of David Lloyd George* (Boston: Little, Brown and Co., 1936), 3:104–6.

22. Sims to Daniels, cable, 1 May 1917, TP File, RG 45.

23. Sims to Daniels, cable, 21 June 1917, TP File, RG 45.

24. Daniels to Sims, cable, 24 June 1917, TP File, RG 45.

25. Sims to Daniels, cable, 29 June 1917, TP File, RG 45.

26. Daniels to Sims, memorandum, 16 July 1917, in Sims, *Victory at Sea*, 391–92.

27. This includes destroyers in commission at that time; see Paul Halpern, *A Naval History of World War I* (Annapolis, Md.: Naval Institute Press, 1994), 359.

28. Michael Simpson, ed., *Documents Relating to Anglo-American Naval Relations, 1917–1919* (Brookfield: Naval Records Society, 1991), 60–63.

29. Simpson, *Anglo-American Naval Relations*, 61n.

30. Churchill (U.S.) to Wilson, July 1917, in Papers of Admiral William S. Sims, Manuscript Division, Library of Congress.

31. Wilson to Daniels, 2 July 1917, TD File, RG 45.

32. Wilson to Sims, 4 July 1917, TD File, RG 45.

33. Sims to Wilson, 12 July 1917, series 2 (microfilm), Papers of President Wilson.

34. Northcliffe to War Cabinet, 5 July 1917, TT File, RG 45.

35. Jellicoe to Northcliffe, 10 July 1917, TT File, RG 45.

36. Daniels to Lansing, 9 July 1917, Papers of Admiral Sims.

37. Sims to Daniels, letter, 16 July 1917, TP File, RG 45.

38. Ibid.

39. Ibid.

40. Jellicoe requested coal-burners because of the serious oil shortage in Britain.

41. Sims to Daniels, cable, 21 July 1917, TT File, RG 45.

42. Gerald Wheeler, *Admiral William Veazie Pratt, U.S. Navy* (Washington, D.C.: Department of the Navy, 1974), 103. Security concerns remained the primary reason for retaining the battleships in U.S. waters.

43. Klachko and Trask, *William Shepherd Benson*, 81.

44. Geddes to Lloyd George, memorandum, 29 August 1917, ADM 116/1804, Admiralty Records.

45. Sims to Pratt, letter, 30 August 1917, in Papers of Admiral William V. Pratt, Operational Archives Branch, U.S. Naval Historical Center, Washington Navy Yard, Washington, D.C.

46. Viscount Jellicoe, *The Crisis of the Naval War* (New York: George Doran Co., 1920), 161.

47. Paul Cronon, *The Cabinet Diaries of Josephus Daniels* (Lincoln: University of Nebraska Press, 1963), entry for 18 September 1917, 203.

48. Klachko and Trask, *William Shepherd Benson*, 81.

49. Mayo to Daniels, "Report of the International Conference Held in London, 4–5 September, and Kindred Matters," memorandum, 8 September 1917, in Papers of Admiral William S. Benson, Manuscript Division, Library of Congress.

50. Mayo to Benson, cable, 5 September 1917, TT File, RG 45.

51. Extract from Admiralty Operations Committee Minutes, 20 September 1917, ADM 137/1420, Admiralty Records.

52. Paolo Coletta, *Sea Power in the Atlantic and Mediterranean in World War I* (New York: University Press of America, 1989), 61–62.

53. "Statement of Admiralty Policy Prepared for Admiral Mayo," 17 November 1917, TT File, RG 45.

54. "Admiral Mayo's General Impressions Regarding Conditions in the Admiralty," memorandum, September 1917, TP File, RG 45.

55. Capt. Dudley Pound to Wemyss, "Cooperation," memorandum, 29 September 1917, ADM 137/1437, Admiralty Records; "Memorandum by Admiral Henry T. Mayo, U.S. Navy, for First Sea Lord," 29 September 1917, ADM 137/1437, Admiralty Records.

56. "Assistance Desired from the United States," Admiralty memorandum, 2 October 1917, G.T.-2164, CAB 24, GT Papers, 1917–1919, War Cabinet, Public Record Office (hereafter cited as War Cabinet); this document is also contained in ADM 137/2710, Admiralty Records.

57. Sims became the commander of U.S. Naval Forces in Europe shortly after his arrival in London.

58. Sims to Pratt, letter, 24 September 1917, TD File, RG 45.

59. Klachko and Trask, *William Shepherd Benson*, 82.

60. Benson to Sims, letter, 24 September 1917, TD File, RG 45.

61. Klachko and Trask, *William Shepherd Benson*, 169–80.

62. First Lord of the Admiralty to Secretary of the Navy, telegram, 13 October 1917, ADM 116/1805, Admiralty Records.

63. Jellicoe to Benson, letter, 22 September 1917, File 677, RG 45.

64. Benson to Jellicoe, letter, 22 October 1917, TT File, RG 45.

65. Sims to Benson, 1 September 1917, Papers of Admiral Benson.

66. Sims to Pratt, letter, 27 September 1917, TD File, RG 45.

67. Allard, "Anglo-American Naval Differences," 77–78.

68. Churchill (U.S.) to Wilson, letter, 22 October 1917, in Simpson, *Anglo-American Naval Relations*, 126.

69. Klachko and Trask, *William Shepherd Benson*, 86.

70. Trask, *Captains and Cabinets*, 174–76.

71. Ibid.

72. Cronon, *Cabinet Diaries of Josephus Daniels*, entry for 10 November 1917, 234.

73. "Memorandum by Admiral Benson," 10 November 1917, Papers of Admiral Benson.

74. Ibid.

75. Daniels to Benson, cable, 13 November 1917, TD File, RG 45.

76. Director of Plans Adm. Roger Keyes, "Co-operation of the British and American Battle Fleets and Suggested Re-distribution of Force," memorandum, 19 November 1917, ADM 137/2704, Admiralty Records.

77. Ibid.

78. Ibid.

79. Simpson, *Anglo-American Naval Relations*, 328.

80. Klachko and Trask, *William Shepherd Benson*, 95–99.

81. Benson, "Naval Policy of the United States," memorandum, November 1917, Papers of Admiral Benson.

82. Trask, *Captains and Cabinets*, 179–80. The armistice came before a joint naval offensive was accomplished.

83. Klachko and Trask, *William Shepherd Benson*, 27–40.

84. As of February 1941, the U.S. Navy became a two-ocean navy with battle fleets in the Atlantic and the Pacific.

Chapter 2 / Learning the Ropes

1. A notable example is O'Connell, *Sacred Vessels*, 153.

2. Sir Frederick Maurice, *Lessons of Allied Cooperation: Naval, Military and Air* (London: Oxford University Press, 1942), 177.

3. Arthur J. Marder, *From the Dreadnought to Scapa Flow: The Royal Navy in the Fisher Era, 1904–1919* (London: Oxford University Press, 1969), 4:42.

4. Beatty to Admiralty, "Situation in the North Sea," memorandum, 9 January 1918, ADM 137/1459, Admiralty Records; Marder, *From the Dreadnought to Scapa Flow*, 5:133–38.

5. Beatty to Admiralty, "Situation in the North Sea."

6. Ibid.

7. Ibid.

8. Wemyss, Admiralty memorandum, 11 January 1918, ADM 137/1459, Admiralty Records.

9. Minutes, 18 January 1918, CAB 23/5, War Cabinet.

10. Marder, *From the Dreadnought to Scapa Flow*, 5:134–35.

11. Vice Adm. John McCrea, oral history transcript, August 1974, number 10-2, 10-3, Naval Institute Oral History Collection, Annapolis, Md.

12. Ibid., number 10-26.

13. "United States Battleships in European Waters," historical narrative, 22 September 1921, OB File, RG 45. For biographical information on Rodman and the battleship captains, see Wheeler, *William Veazie Pratt*, 103, 254.

14. Papers of Secretary of the Navy Josephus Daniels, Manuscript Division, Li-

brary of Congress; Daniels's papers contain very few references to U.S. battleship operations. See also Papers of President Wilson.

15. Sims originally went to London as only a liaison with the Admiralty, but he soon became the commander in chief of U.S. Forces.

16. Rodman explained his wartime orders and the chain of command in testimony before a Senate subcommittee; see Senate Committee on Naval Affairs, *Hearings before the Subcommittee of the Committee on Naval Affairs,* 66th Cong., 2d sess., 7 April 1920, 857.

17. Henry A. Wiley, *An Admiral from Texas* (New York: Doubleday, Doran and Co., 1934), 185–89; see also Rodman to Mayo, "Division Nine: Synopsis of Events since Departure from the United States," memorandum, 19 December 1917, OB File, RG 45.

18. McCrea, oral history transcript, August 1974, number 11-17.

19. Wiley, *An Admiral from Texas,* 188–90.

20. "History of U.S.S. *Delaware* during the World War," historical narrative, entry for 2 July 1919, OS File, RG 45.

21. Wiley, *An Admiral from Texas,* 185–87.

22. E. B. Potter, *The Naval Academy Illustrated History of the United States Navy* (New York: Thomas Crowell Co., 1971), 141.

23. A. A. Hoehling, *The Great War at Sea: A History of Naval Action, 1914–1918* (New York: Galahad Books, 1965), 247n. This story may be spurious, but it is in keeping with Rodman's character. The admiral disliked paperwork and left behind few personal papers.

24. War Diary, Division Nine, U.S. Atlantic Fleet, entry for 14 December 1917, OB File, RG 45. In U.S. naval correspondence, these ships continued to be called Division Nine. In the Grand Fleet, they were officially Division Eight and the Sixth Squadron. Informally, they were called "the American squadron" or "the United States squadron."

25. Trask, *Captains and Cabinets,* 364.

26. Randal Gray, ed., *Conway's All the World's Fighting Ships, 1906–1921* (Annapolis, Md.: Naval Institute Press, 1985), 21–36, 110–15.

27. Gray, *Conway's, 1906–1921,* 113; Paul Silverstone, *U.S. Warships of World War I* (Garden City: Doubleday and Co., 1970), 44–45.

28. Hugh Rodman, *Yarns of a Kentucky Admiral* (Indianapolis: Bobbs-Merrill Co., 1928), 268–69.

29. Memorandum, Admiralty to Beatty, 22 November 1917, ADM 137/1896, Admiralty Records.

30. Memorandum, Admiralty to Beatty, 6 December 1917, ADM 137/1896, Admiralty Records. This memorandum includes instructions on supplying the Americans with signal books, ciphers, and navigation information.

31. McCrea, oral history transcript, August 1974, number 11-27.

32. "Grand Fleet Battle Instructions," 1 January 1918, ADM 116/1342, Admiralty Records; Marder, *From the Dreadnought to Scapa Flow*, 4:30–31.

33. Instructions for the Fifth and Sixth Battle Squadrons, in "Grand Fleet Battle Instructions."

34. Ibid.

35. Ibid.

36. Wiley, *An Admiral from Texas*, 190–91.

37. Rodman, *Yarns of a Kentucky Admiral*, 268–69.

38. Beatty to Admiralty, cable, 6 January 1918, ADM 137/1964, Admiralty Records; Admiralty to Beatty, cable, 7 January 1918, ADM 137/1964, Admiralty Records.

39. Rodman, *Yarns of a Kentucky Admiral*, 274–75.

40. "Historical Sketch of the U.S.S. *Florida*," historical narrative, n.d., OS File, RG 45.

41. Rodman to Secretary of the Navy (Operations), "Report of Battle Practices of Division Nine and Battle Squadrons of the Grand Fleet," 25 February 1918, OB File, RG 45.

42. Ibid.

43. Steven Roskill, *Admiral of the Fleet Earl Beatty: The Last Naval Hero* (New York: Atheneum, 1981), 243–44.

44. King George V to Beatty, letter, 10 February 1918, in Bryan Ranft, ed., *The Beatty Papers: The Private and Official Correspondence of Admiral of the Fleet Earl Beatty* (Brookfield, Vt.: Scholarly Press, 1989), 511.

45. Wemyss's concern for the Dover Patrol was justified; on 14 February, German destroyers severely mauled the drifters of the Dover Patrol. See Sir William Corbett and Henry Newbolt, *History of the Great War: Naval Operations* (New York: Longman, Green and Co., 1931), 5:209–20.

46. Wemyss to Beatty, letter, 28 January 1918, in Papers of Lord Wester Wemyss, Special Collections, University of California, Irvine (microfilm).

47. Beatty to Wemyss, letter, 31 January 1918, Papers of Lord Wemyss.

48. Beatty to Grand Fleet, "Operation EC 1," memorandum, 28 January 1918, ADM 137/2025, Admiralty Records.

49. Rodman to Secretary of the Navy (Operations), general report, 2 February 1918, OB File, RG 45.

50. Rodman to Daniels, general report, 9 February 1918, OB File, RG 45.

51. Beatty to his wife, letter, 5 February 1918, in Ranft, *The Beatty Papers*, 508.

52. "The North Sea," Admiralty historical narrative, postwar undated, ADM 116/3399, Admiralty Records. During these months, 6,475 vessels were convoyed, with a loss of 1.15 percent.

53. Sir Archibald Hurd, *History of the Great War: The Merchant Navy* (London: John Murray, 1929), 3:67.

54. Newbolt, *Naval Operations*, 5:153. Newbolt erroneously reports a speed of 34 knots for *Brummer* and *Bremse*; compare Gray, *Conway's, 1906–1921*, 162.

55. Newbolt, *Naval Operations*, 5:154–55.

56. "Draft Statement for First Lord," n.d., ADM 116/1806, Admiralty Records; Hurd, *The Merchant Navy*, 3:73.

57. Halpern, *A Naval History*, 403.

58. Beatty to Admiralty, "Notes on Conference with D.C.N.S. [Deputy Chief of Naval Staff] on 25 February 1918," 7 March 1918, ADM 137/1646, Admiralty Records.

59. Newbolt, *Naval Operations*, 5:194. Newbolt comments that this radical departure from doctrine shows the extent that the war on commerce engaged naval resources. Halpern quotes Newbolt in his discussion of the Scandinavian convoy, see *A Naval History*, 379.

60. "Operation 'Z.6,'" orders, 3 February 1918, ADM 137/2025, Admiralty Records; Rodman to Beatty, "Report Regarding Convoy Duty," memorandum, 10 February 1918, ADM 137/877, Admiralty Records.

61. It was later established that this was probably the British airship C-18 out of Peterhead; perhaps the airship was marking the position of the returning covering force for convoy "HZ6"; Beatty to Rodman, "Proceedings of Sixth Battle Squadron, 6–10 February," memorandum, 14 February 1918, ADM 137/877, Admiralty Records.

62. Rodman to Secretary of the Navy (Operations), general report, 9 February 1918, OB File, RG 45; Rodman, "Report Regarding Convoy Duty."

63. H. A. Scales (*Delaware*) to Rodman, "Submarine Attack on *Delaware*, February 8th, 1918," n.d., OS File, RG 45; Thomas Washington (*Florida*) to Rodman, "Submarine Attack on February 8, 1918," 10 February 1918, OS File, RG 45.

64. "Historical Sketch of the U.S.S. *Florida*"; Rodman to Secretary of the Navy (Operations), report, 9 February 1918, OB File, RG 45; Rodman, "Report Regarding Convoy Duty."

65. Wiley, *An Admiral from Texas*, 201.

66. Rodman to Secretary of the Navy (Operations), report, 9 February 1918, OB File, RG 45; Rodman, "Report Regarding Convoy Duty."

67. War Journals, U-80 and U-82, entries for 8 February 1918, Microfilm Publication T-1022, Records of the German Navy, 1850–1945, RG 242, National Archives Branch Depository, College Park, Md. (hereafter cited as Records of the German Navy). The official German history of naval operations in the North Sea, which includes detailed accounts of individual U-boat operations and even unsuccessful attacks on warships, does not mention any encounter; see Walther Gladisch and Otto Groos, *Der Krieg in der Nordsee: 1918* (Berlin: E. S. Mittler, 1930), vol. 7.

68. Rodman to Commander in Chief, Atlantic Fleet (Mayo), "Division Nine: Synopsis of Events since Departure from the United States," memorandum, 19 December 1917, OB File, RG 45; Sims to Benson, 20 December 1917, cable, OB File, RG 45.

69. Sims to Rodman, memorandum, 20 December 1917, TD File, RG 45. The Admiralty Plans Division and American Planning Section in London drafted several proposals that included basing U.S. battleships in Norway, but U.S. planning never went any further than that.

70. Benson to Sims, cable, 5 January 1918, OB File, RG 45.

71. Sims to Benson, cable, 8 January 1918, OB File, RG 45.

72. "Historical Sketch of the U.S.S. *Texas* during the World War," historical narrative, 4 September 1923, OS File, RG 45.

73. Adm. Bernhard H. Bieri, oral history transcript, n.d., number 1-41, Naval Institute Oral History Collection, Annapolis, Md.

74. Instructions for Distribution of Fire, in "Grand Fleet Battle Instructions."

75. Rodman to Secretary of the Navy, memorandum, 28 September 1918, OB File, RG 45. Rodman sent a summary of the above to Sims in a memorandum of the same date, also in the OB File.

76. Captain Aylmer, R.N., to Captain of the Fleet, memorandum, 2 March 1918, ADM 137/1898, Admiralty Records.

77. Sims to Benson, cable, 10 March 1918, OB File, RG 45.

78. Sims to Daniels, memorandum, 11 March 1918, OB File, RG 45.

79. "Historical Sketch of the U.S.S. *Florida*."

80. Rodman to Sims, "Statement of Naval Accomplishments for Publicity Purposes," memorandum, 23 May 1918, OB File, RG 45.

81. Scales (*Delaware*) to Rodman, report, 19 February 1918, OS File, RG 45.

82. Rodman to Secretary of the Navy (Operations), general report, 23 February 1918, OB File, RG 45.

83. Rodman, *Yarns of a Kentucky Admiral*, 286.

84. Scales (*Delaware*) to Rodman, report, 16 February 1918, OS File, RG 45.

85. Rodman to Secretary of the Navy (Operations), general report, 23 February 1918, OB File, RG 45.

86. Rodman to Secretary of the Navy (Operations), general report, 2 March 1918, OB File, RG 45.

87. Beatty to Admiralty, "Notes on Conference with the Deputy Chief of the Naval Staff on 25 February 1918," memorandum, 7 March 1918, ADM 137/1646, Admiralty Records.

88. War Cabinet 377, 29 March 1918, CAB 23/2, War Cabinet.

89. Both Halpern and Marder comment on the fine working relationship between Beatty and Rodman despite Beatty's poor appraisal of the American's gunnery.

90. Wiley, *An Admiral from Texas*, 192.

91. Ibid., 198–99.

92. Beatty to Rodman, "Operation 'Z.15,'" orders, 6 March 1918, ADM 137/877, Admiralty Records.

93. Rodman to Beatty, report, 13 March 1918, OB File, RG 45; Rodman to Secretary of the Navy (Operations), general report, 16 March 1918, OB File, RG 45.

94. Rodman to Beatty, report, 13 March 1918, OB File, RG 45; Rodman to Secretary of the Navy (Operations), general report, 16 March 1918, OB File, RG 45.

95. Benson to Sims, cable, 15 March 1918, CB File, RG 45.

96. Sims to Benson, cable, 17 March 1918, CB File, RG 45.

97. Beatty to Rodman, "Operation 'Z.25,'" orders, 15 April 1918, ADM 137/1990, Admiralty Records; "Historical Sketch of the U.S.S. *Florida*."

98. U-boat war journals, entries for 17 April 1918, Records of the German Navy. None of the U-boats operating in the area reported sighting any warships.

99. Rodman to Beatty, report, 20 April 1918, ADM 137/877, Admiralty Reports; Rodman to Secretary of the Navy (Operations), general report, 20 April 1918, OB File, RG 45.

100. Newbolt, *Naval Operations*, 5:230–40.

101. Ibid.

102. Ibid., 5:417–20.

103. "Historical sketch of the U.S.S. *Florida.*"

104. Halpern, *A Naval History*, 419.

105. "History of U.S.S. *Delaware* during the World War," historical narrative, entry for 16 July 1919, OS File, RG 45.

106. Rodman, *Yarns of a Kentucky Admiral*, 270–71.

107. Marder, *From the Dreadnought to Scapa Flow*, 5:148–49.

108. Newbolt, *Naval Operations*, 5:230.

109. Halpern, *A Naval History*, 420.

110. Rodman to Secretary of the Navy (Operations), general report, 27 April 1918, quoted in Sims to Benson, memorandum, 2 May 1918, TD File, RG 45.

111. Sims to Rodman, letter, 2 May 1918, Papers of Admiral Sims.

112. Sims to Benson, letter, 2 May 1918, TD File, RG 45.

113. Rodman's available correspondence and reports do not record his ever pursuing the matter again.

114. Halpern, *A Naval History*, 379.

115. Beatty to Admiralty, memorandum, 3 February 1918, Papers of Admiral Sims.

116. Sims to Rodman, letter, 18 February 1918, Papers of Admiral Sims.

117. Sims to Rodman, letter, 23 April 1918, Papers of Admiral Sims.

118. Ibid.

119. Trask, *Captains and Cabinets*, 193–94.

120. Klachko and Trask, *William Shepherd Benson*, 96.

121. Daniels later revealed that an unidentified naval officer told him he had earned the "everlasting enmity" of Admiral Sims for blocking the appointment; Josephus Daniels, *The Wilson Years*, 495.

122. McCrea, oral history transcript, August 1974, number 12-2.

123. "The Future of the Russian Fleets," Admiralty memorandum, 25 April 1918, G.T.-4344, CAB 24/49, War Cabinet.

124. "Redistribution of Naval Forces in the Mediterranean," Admiralty memorandum, 29 April 1918, G.T.-4393, CAB 24/49, War Cabinet.

125. War Cabinet 401, 30 April 1918, and War Cabinet 405, 6 May 1918, CAB 23/6, War Cabinet.

126. Halpern, *A Naval History*, 400–1.

127. Marder, *From the Dreadnought to Scapa Flow*, 4:25.

128. Fortunately for the Allies, the Treaty of Brest-Litovsk provided that the

Russian Black Sea Fleet would remain Russian, and so redistribution of naval forces in the Mediterranean became a moot point.

129. Rodman to Secretary of the Navy (Operations), general report, 19 May 1918, OB File, RG 45.

130. Plans Division to Admiralty, "Concentration of the U.S.A. Battle Fleet in the North Sea," memorandum, 5 June 1918, ADM 137/2709, Admiralty Records.

131. Rodman to Secretary of the Navy (Operations), general report, 23 March 1918, OB File, RG 45.

132. Rodman to Secretary of the Navy (Operations), general report, 4 May 1918, OB File, RG 45.

133. Rodman to Secretary of the Navy (Operations), general report, 29 June 1918, OB File, RG 45.

Chapter 3 / Earning Respect

1. Rodman to Secretary of the Navy (Operations), general report, 6 July 1918, OB File, RG 45.

2. Beatty to Rodman, "Operation M.4," orders, 26 June 1918, ADM 137/1963, Admiralty Records.

3. Halpern, *A Naval History*, 438–41.

4. War Diary, Ninth Division, U.S. Atlantic Fleet, entry for 30 June 1918, OS File, RG 45.

5. Rodman to Beatty, report, 2 July 1918, ADM 137/1963, Admiralty Records; Rodman to Secretary of the Navy (Operations), general report, 13 July 1918, OB File, RG 45.

6. War Journal, U-70, entry for 30 June 1918, Records of the German Navy.

7. Rodman to Secretary of the Navy (Operations), general report, 13 July 1918, OB File, RG 45; Wiley, *An Admiral from Texas*, 206–7.

8. Beatty to Rodman, "Operation M.4," addendum to orders, 29 June 1918, ADM 137/1963, Admiralty Records; Rodman to Secretary of the Navy (Operations), general report, 6 July 1918, OB File, RG 45.

9. McCrea, oral history transcript, August 1974, number 13-7.

10. Rodman to Secretary of the Navy (Operations), general report, 6 July 1918, OB File, RG 45; Rodman to Secretary of the Navy (Operations), general report, 13 July 1918, OB File, RG 45.

11. Rodman to Secretary of the Navy (Operations), general report, 27 April 1918, OB File, RG 45.

12. Rodman to Secretary of the Navy (Operations), general report, 15 June 1918, OB File, RG 45.

13. Beatty to Grand Fleet, "Grand Fleet Boxing Championship, 1918," memorandum, 25 July 1918, ADM 137/2026, Admiralty Records; War Diary, USS *New York*, undated excerpt, OB File, RG 45.

14. War Diary, USS *New York*, undated excerpt, OB File, RG 45.

15. Ibid.

16. Rodman to Secretary of the Navy, general report, 13 July 1918, OB File, RG 45.

17. Beatty to Grand Fleet, "Visit of His Majesty the King," memorandum, 19 July 1918, ADM 137/2026, Admiralty Records.

18. Rodman, *Yarns of a Kentucky Admiral*, 275–77.

19. Beatty to Grand Fleet, memorandum, 24 July 1918, ADM 137/2026, Admiralty Records.

20. McCrea, oral history transcript, August 1974, number 13-30.

21. Benson to Sims, cable, 14 July 1918, OS File, RG 45.

22. Bullard to Rodman, report, 29 July 1918, OS File, RG 45.

23. U-boat war journals, entries for 28 July 1918, Records of the German Navy.

24. Rodman to Beatty, memorandum, 29 July 1918, ADM 137/1935, Admiralty Records; Historical Narrative, "History of U.S.S. *Delaware* during the World War," entry for 2 July 1919, OS File, RG 45.

25. Beatty to relevant fleet commanders, "Operation 'M.9,'" orders, 6 August 1918, ADM 137/2026, Admiralty Records.

26. Rodman to Beatty, report, 11 August 1918, ADM 137/1963, Admiralty Records.

27. Evan-Thomas to Captain (D) XVth Destroyer Flotilla, memorandum, 14 August 1918, ADM 137/1963, Admiralty Records.

28. Captain (D) XVth Flotilla to Evan-Thomas, report, 14 August 1918, ADM 137/1963, Admiralty Records. Reports from the destroyer captains are included.

29. Ibid.

30. Beatty to Evan-Thomas, memorandum, 20 August 1918, ADM 137/1963, Admiralty Records.

31. U-boat war journals, entries for 8 August 1918, Records of the German Navy.

32. War Diary, USS *New York*, undated excerpts, OB File, RG 45.

33. Rodman to Secretary of the Navy (Operations), general report, 9 March 1918, OB File, RG 45.

34. Rodman to Secretary of the Navy (Operations), general report, 6 April 1918, OB File, RG 45.

35. Rodman to Secretary of the Navy (Operations), general report, 13 July 1918, OB File, RG 45.

36. Norman Friedman, *U.S. Battleships: An Illustrated Design History*, 179; Halpern, *A Naval History*, 441–43.

37. Beatty to Grand Fleet, "Remarks on Tactical Exercise Carried Out on 24 September, 1918," memorandum, 28 October 1918, ADM 137/2026, Admiralty Records; Beatty to Grand Fleet, "Distribution of Fire Exercise," memorandum, 27 September 1918, ADM 137/2026, Admiralty Records.

38. Beatty to Grand Fleet, "Remarks on Tactical Exercise Carried Out on 24 September 1918," memorandum, 28 October 1918, ADM 137/2026, Admiralty Records; Beatty to Grand Fleet, "Distribution of Fire Exercise," memorandum, 27 September 1918, ADM 137/2026, Admiralty Records.

39. Robert Love recounts this example, but he erroneously states that Beatty sent the U.S. battleships to Berehaven, Ireland, during this alarm; Robert Love, Jr., *History of the U.S. Navy, 1775–1941* (Harrisburg: Stockpole Books, 1992), 2:505.

40. Rodman to Secretary of the Navy (Operations), general report, 19 October 1918, OB File, RG 45.

41. The German official history of naval operations in the North Sea makes no mention of any raider sortie into the North Sea at this time; Gladisch and Groos, *Der Krieg in der Nordsee*, vol. 7.

42. Rodman to Secretary of the Navy (Operations), general report, 19 October 1918, OB File, RG 45.

43. U-boat war journals, entries for 14 October 1918, Records of the German Navy; Gray, *Conway's, 1906–1921*, 173–81.

44. German records make no mention of an attack, but it is possible that one of the UB-boats lost around this time could have been responsible for the attack.

45. Rodman to Secretary of the Navy (Operations), general report, 19 October 1918, OB File, RG 45; also see a series of cables between the commander of the Second Battle Cruiser Squadron and Beatty, 14 and 15 October 1918, ADM 127/1973, Admiralty Records.

46. Rodman to Secretary of the Navy (Director of Gunnery and Engineering), report, 20 October 1918, OS File, RG 45.

47. Ibid.

48. Rodman to Secretary of the Navy (Operations), general report, 9 November 1918, OB File, RG 45.

49. McCrea, oral history transcript, 1 October 1974, number 14-1.

50. Rodman to Sims, general reports, 26 October, 2 November, and 9 November 1918, OB File, RG 45.

51. James Stokesbury, *A Short History of World War I* (New York: William Morrow and Co., 1981), 281–307; Halpern, *A Naval History*, 444.

52. Holger Herwig, *Luxury Fleet: The Imperial German Navy, 1888–1918* (London: Ashfield Press, 1980), 247–48.

53. Ibid.

54. Herwig, *Luxury Fleet*, 249–54.

55. Halpern, *A Naval History*, 447; Klachko and Trask, *William Shepherd Benson*, 127–38.

56. Joubert McCrea to his parents, letter, 12 November 1918, U.S. Army Military Institute, Carlisle Barracks, Pa. Joubert McCrea was apparently not closely related to Vice Adm. John McCrea.

57. Marder, *From the Dreadnought to Scapa Flow*, 5:189.

58. Beatty to Grand Fleet, "Visit of Their Majesties the King and Queen and His Royal Highness the Prince of Wales," memorandum, 19 November 1918, ADM 137/2026, Admiralty Records.

59. Rodman to Secretary of the Navy (Operations), general report, 23 November 1918, OB File, RG 45; Beatty to Grand Fleet, "Operation ZZ," memorandum, 20 November 1918, ADM 137/2026, Admiralty Records.

60. Rodman to Secretary of the Navy (Operations), general report, 23 November 1918, OB File, RG 45; Marder, *From the Dreadnought to Scapa Flow*, 5:190.

61. Rodman to Secretary of the Navy (Operations), general report, 23 November 1918, OB File, RG 45.

62. Marder, *From the Dreadnought to Scapa Flow*, 5:191.

63. Beatty to Grand Fleet, memorandum, 21 November 1918, ADM 137/2026, Admiralty Records.

64. Joubert McCrea, diary entry for 21 November 1918, U.S. Army Military Institute, Carlisle Barracks, Pa.

65. Wemyss, unpublished memoirs, quoted in Marder, *From the Dreadnought to Scapa Flow*, 5:165.

66. Bieri, oral history transcript, number 1-49.

67. Beatty to Sixth Battle Squadron, farewell address in "General Bulletin No. 24," 10 December 1918, Papers of Admiral Benson.

68. Rodman to Beatty, letter, 30 November 1918, Papers of Admiral of the Fleet Earl David Beatty, National Maritime Museum, Greenwich, U.K.

69. Beatty to Sixth Battle Squadron, naval signal, 1 December 1918, ADM 137/1964, Admiralty Records.

70. Sixth Battle Squadron to Beatty, naval signal, 1 December 1918, ADM 137/1964, Admiralty Records.

71. Rodman, *Yarns of a Kentucky Admiral*, 267.

72. Chatfield is quoted in Marder, *From the Dreadnought to Scapa Flow*, 5:125.

73. McCrea, oral history transcript, 1 October 1974, number 14-10.

Chapter 4 / Lessons Learned

1. Elting Morison, *Admiral Sims and the Modern American Navy* (Boston: Houghton Mifflin Co., 1942), 242.

2. Peter Padfield, *Guns at Sea* (New York: St. Martin's Press, 1974), 245–54.

3. Ibid.

4. Ibid., 252.

5. Gunnery Officers of Battleship Division Nine, report, January 1919, *Monthly Information Bulletin*, Office of Naval Intelligence, Operational Archives Branch, U.S. Naval War College.

6. Friedman, *U.S. Battleships*, 170–87; Norman Friedman, *U.S. Naval Weapon Systems: Every Gun, Mine, and Torpedo Used by the U.S. Navy from 1883 to the Present* (Annapolis, Md.: Naval Institute Press, 1983), 25–33.

7. Jon Sumida, "British Capital Ship Design and Fire Control in the *Dreadnought* Era: Sir John Fisher, Arthur Hungerford Pollen, and the Battle Cruiser," *Journal of Modern History* 51 (June 1979): 225; also see his *In Defense of Naval Supremacy: Finance, Technology and British Naval Policy, 1889–1914* (Boston: Unwin Hyman, 1989).

8. Padfield, *Guns at Sea*, 250.

9. Friedman, *U.S. Naval Weapon Systems*, 31–33.

10. Gunnery Officers, Battleship Division Nine, "Comparison of British and American Gunnery Training, Fire Control, Control of Searchlights, and Control Stations," report, February 1919, *Monthly Information Bulletin*, Office of Naval Intelligence.

11. Friedman, *U.S. Naval Weapon Systems*, 31–33.

12. Kinkaid to Secretary of the Navy, memorandum, 28 February 1918, 44:32,

Record Group 74, Bureau of Ordnance Papers, National Archives (hereafter cited as Ordnance Papers).

13. Lt. Cdr. C. H. Jones, "Modern Fire Control Installation," lecture, 23 February 1926, XOGF 1926–68, U.S. Naval War College.

14. Bureau of Ordnance to Director of Naval Intelligence, memorandum, 11 February 1914, 28499, Box 345, Ordnance Papers.

15. Earle to Daniels, memorandum, 6 July 1917, 28499, Box 345, Ordnance Papers.

16. Earle to Pollen, letter, 19 November 1917, 28499, Box 345, Ordnance Papers.

17. Pollen to Earle, letter, 27 November 1917, 28499, Box 345, Ordnance Papers.

18. Commanding Officer, *Louisiana*, to Commander Force One, report, 31 March 1919, 28499, Box 345, Ordnance Papers.

19. Earle to Pollen, letter, 7 November 1918, 28499, Box 345, Ordnance Papers.

20. Rodman to Secretary of the Navy (Operations), general report, 24 August 1918, OB File, RG 45.

21. Rodman to Secretary of the Navy (Operations), general report, 9 February 1918, OB File, RG 45.

22. Rodman to Secretary of the Navy (Operations), general report, 24 August 1918, OB File, RG 45.

23. Rodman to Secretary of the Navy (Operations), general report, 16 March 1918, OB File, RG 45.

24. Friedman, *U.S. Battleships*, 176.

25. Nathan Miller, *The U.S. Navy: An Illustrated History* (New York: Bonanza Books, 1977), 264.

26. McCrea, oral history transcript, August 1974, number 11-6.

27. Senate Committee on Naval Affairs, *Hearings before the Subcommittee of the Committee on Naval Affairs*, 66th Cong., 2nd sess., 7 April 1920, 858–63.

28. Rodman to Secretary of the Navy, "Report of Battle Practices of Division Nine and Battle Squadrons of the Grand Fleet," report, 25 February 1918, OB File, RG 45.

29. Rodman to Secretary of the Navy (Operations), general report, 4 May 1918, OB File, RG 45.

30. Rodman to Secretary of the Navy (Operations), general report, 2 February 1918, OB File, RG 45; Sims to Rodman, letter, 11 July 1918, Papers of Admiral Sims.

31. Mayo to Secretary of the Navy (Operations), "Inspection of Battleship Division Nine," report, 1 November 1918, OB File, RG 45.

32. Mayo to Secretary of the Navy (Operations), "Gunnery: Methods and Appliances," report, 18 June 1919. This study was based on inspections, conferences, and interviews of both U.S. and British officers between September and December 1918. Benson forwarded a copy to the General Board; see GB File 436, Records of the General Board of the Navy, Subject File 1911–1927, RG 80, National Archives.

33. Rodman to Secretary of the Navy (Operations), general report, 23 February 1918, OB File, RG 45.

34. Rodman to Secretary of the Navy (Operations), "Training under War Conditions in War Zone," general report, 15 June 1918, OB File, RG 45.

35. W. H. P. Blandy, "Possible Improvements in Our Gunnery Training," U.S. Naval Institute *Proceedings* 51 (December 1925): 1696–1702.

36. William S. Sims, "Battle Practice, U.S. Navy," memorandum, UNOPG, 1916–69, U.S. Naval War College.

37. Kinkaid to Secretary of the Navy, memorandum, 28 February 1918, 44:32, Ordnance Papers.

38. Rodman to Secretary of the Navy (Operations), general report, 2 March 1918, OB File, RG 45.

39. Senate Committee on Naval Affairs, *Hearings before the Subcommittee of the Committee on Naval Affairs*, 66th Cong., 2d sess., 7 April 1920, 858–60.

40. NHC Pamphlet, "Orders for Gunnery Exercises: Battle Practices for All Classes of Vessels, 1918–1919," U.S. Naval War College.

41. Commander in Chief, Atlantic Fleet, to Chief of Naval Operations, memorandum, 29 September 1921, UNOPG 1921-168, Naval War College.

42. Capt. Chauncey Shackford, "Naval Gunnery," lecture, 19 January 1923, XOGG 1923-44, Naval War College.

43. Cdr. Henry K. Hewitt, "Naval Gunnery: 1925," lecture, 24 July 1925, XOGF 1925-127, Naval War College.

44. Richard Down to M. E. Browning, Commander in Chief, North America and West Indies, forwarded to the Admiralty, report, 5 July 1917, ADM 137/1621, Admiralty Records.

45. Chauncey Shackford, "Naval Gunnery," lecture, 19 January 1923, XOGG 1923-44, Naval War College.

46. Rodman to Secretary of the Navy (Operations), "Report of the Battle Practices of Division Nine and Battle Squadrons of the Grand Fleet," 25 February 1918, OB File, RG 45.

47. Kinkaid to Secretary of the Navy, memorandum, 28 February 1918, 44:32, Ordnance Papers.

48. Rodman to Secretary of the Navy (Operations), general report, 19 October 1918, OB File, RG 45.

49. Mayo to Secretary of the Navy (Bureau of Ordnance, Construction and Repair, Steam and Engineering), "Remarks on Full Caliber Practice (Second Battle Squadron), 28 September 1918," memorandum, n.d., GB 436, RG 80.

50. Rodman to Secretary of the Navy (Operations), general report, 6 July 1918, OB File, RG 45.

51. Capt. R. M. Brainard, "Naval Guns and Fire Control," lecture, 30 March 1923, XOGG 1923, Naval War College.

52. Hewitt, "Naval Gunnery: 1925."

Chapter 5 / Defending the Transatlantic Convoys

1. Halpern, *A Naval History,* 427–29.

2. These raiders sank only about 268,000 tons in 1917, but because of the shortage of shipping and the diversion of cruisers to bring the raiders to bay, their cruises were an operational success; see Halpern, *A Naval History,* 375.

3. Battle cruisers evolved from armored cruisers; they carried the same caliber main battery as battleships, but were more lightly armored and faster, serving as the scouting force of the battle fleet.

4. Admiralty Plans Division, "Appreciation of the Situation as Regards German Raiders," memorandum, 19 November 1917, ADM 137/2704, Admiralty Records.

5. Admiralty to Commo. Gaunt, "For Chief of Naval Operations," cable, 17 December 1917, TP File, RG 45. A pre-dreadnought is any battleship armed with mixed calibers, rather than an all-big-gun ship; HMS *Dreadnought,* with a single-caliber main battery, made all battleships with mixed batteries obsolete by eliminating intermediate calibers.

6. Sims to Benson, cable, 18 December 1917, TP File, RG 45.

7. Benson to Sims, cable, 20 December 1917, TP File, RG 45.

8. The Plans Division was a formal department of the Admiralty; the American planning section was a temporary, less formal staff of U.S. Navy officers who worked with the Plans Division to formulate joint planning.

9. Admiralty Plans Division, "Proposed Measures to be Taken if Enemy Battle Cruisers Enter Atlantic," memorandum, n.d., P.D. 80, ADM 137/2710, Admiralty Records.

10. Admiralty Plans Division, U.S. planning section, "Battle Cruiser Raid," memorandum, 17 May 1918, Memo. No. 26, ADM 137/2710, Admiralty Records.

11. Benson to Sims, cable, 2 July 1918, TD File, RG 45.

12. Sims to Benson, cable, 2 July 1918, TD File, RG 45.

13. Benson to Sims, cable, 31 July 1918, reproduced in U.S. Navy Department, Office of Naval Intelligence Historical Section, *The American Naval Planning Section in London* (Washington, D.C.: GPO, 1923), 352–53.

14. Division Six of the Atlantic Fleet should not be confused with the American squadron (the Sixth Battle Squadron) serving with the Grand Fleet.

15. Benson to Sims, cable, 31 July 1918, in U.S. Navy Department, *The American Naval Planning Section in London*, 352–53.

16. Sims to Benson, cable, 3 August 1918, TP File, RG 45; Sims to Benson, cable, 10 August 1918, TD File, RG 45.

17. Director of Plans to Deputy First Sea Lord, memorandum, 13 August 1918, ADM 137/2710, Admiralty Records.

18. Sims reported the Admiralty's views on this matter in a cable, Sims to Benson, 17 August 1918, CB File, RG 45.

19. Admiralty Plans Division, "Instructions for Guidance in the Event of an Enemy Battle Cruiser Making a Raid in the Atlantic," memorandum, 5 August 1918, P.D. 100, ADM 137/2710, Admiralty Records.

20. Ibid.

21. U.S. Navy Historical Section, "United States Battleships in European Waters Including United States Battleships Attached to the British Grand Fleet," historical narrative, 22 September 1918, OB File, RG 45.

22. Sims to Rodgers, letter, 20 August 1918, TD File, RG 45.

23. Benson to Sims, cable, 31 August 1918, CB File, RG 45.

24. Sims to Benson, cable, 31 August 1918, CB File, RG 45.

25. Halpern, *A Naval History*, 363.

26. Benson to Sims, cable, 3 September 1918, TP File, RG 45. Sims finally issued instructions based on Benson's cable to Division Six in a letter, Sims to Rodgers, 18 September 1918, CB File, RG 45.

27. Admiralty Plans Division, U.S. planning section, and Admiralty Director of Mercantile Movements, "Proposals for Dealing with Convoys During a Battle Cruiser Raid in the Atlantic," memorandum, 4 September 1918, ADM 137/2710, Admiralty Records. Sims recommended the adoption of this plan in a cable, Sims to Benson, 10 September 1918, CB File, RG 45; another copy of this is in a memo from F. H. Schofield of the American planning section to C. T. M. Fuller of the Admiralty Plans Division, ADM 137/2710, Admiralty Records.

28. "Conference Held at Navy Department, Washington, on 10th October, to

Discuss Question of Protection to be Given to Convoys in the Event of a Battle Cruiser Raid in the Atlantic" and "Plan of Action to be Taken in the Event of a Battle Cruiser Raid in the Atlantic: To Be Known as Plan BCR," minutes, 10 October 1918, ADM 137/2710, Admiralty Records. Copies of Plan BCR are in a memorandum, Benson to Sims, 16 October 1918, TP File, RG 45, and in an Admiralty memorandum, 4 November 1918, ADM 137/2710, Admiralty Records.

Chapter 6 / Sentinels

1. "United States Battleships in European Waters Including United States Battleships Attached to the British Grand Fleet"; Rodgers to Sims, memorandum, 25 August 1918, OS File, RG 45.

2. McCrea, oral history transcript, August 1974, number 9-13.

3. Gray, *Conway's, 1906–1921,* 115–16. *Utah,* a coal-burner launched in 1909, was the sister ship of *Florida.*

4. Sims to Rodgers, letter, 10 August 1918, quoted in Sims to Secretary of the Admiralty, memorandum, 19 August 1918, OB File, RG 45.

5. Admiralty to Bayly, memorandum, 21 August 1918, ADM 137/1899, Admiralty Records.

6. Michael Simpson, "Admiral William S. Sims, U.S. Navy, and Admiral Sir Lewis Bayly, Royal Navy: An Unlikely Friendship and Anglo-American Cooperation, 1917–1919," *Naval War College Review* (Spring 1988): 66–80. Sims visited Queenstown on a regular basis because of the U.S. forces there.

7. Sims to Bayly, letter, 20 August 1918, OB File, RG 45. The instructions included parts of the Navy Department's plan against German raiders and instructions regarding the chain of command.

8. Rodgers to Division Six, memorandum, 1 September 1918, IA File, RG 45.

9. Bayly to Rodgers, memorandum, 2 September 1918, ADM 137/1622, Admiralty Records.

10. Rodgers to Sims, general report, 5 September 1918, CB File, RG 45. The purpose of Mayo's visit was to inspect all U.S. Navy operations and facilities in Europe.

11. "United States Battleships in European Waters Including United States Battleships Attached to the British Grand Fleet"; Benson to Sims, cable, 27 August 1918, OS File, RG 45.

12. Rodgers to Sims, memorandum, 12 September 1918, CB File, RG 45.

13. Sims to Rodgers, memorandum, 16 September 1918, CB File, RG 45.

14. Rodgers to Division Six, memorandum, 9 September 1918, OB File, RG 45.

15. Rodgers to Sims, letter, 20 September 1918, Papers of Admiral Sims.

16. Sims to Rodgers, letter, 25 September 1918, Papers of Admiral Sims.

17. Rodgers to Sims, general report, 27 September 1918, OB File, RG 45.

18. Rodgers to Sims, general report, 19 September 1918, OB File, RG 45.

19. Captain Bristol (*Oklahoma*) to Rodgers, "Report of the Burning of the Kite Balloon of the *Utah*," report, 7 October 1918, OS File, RG 45; Rodgers to Sims, general report, 9 October 1918, OB File, RG 45.

20. Rodgers to Sims, general report, 17 October 1918, OB File, RG 45.

21. The American squadron with the Grand Fleet also sortied in search of the raiders, as described in chapter three.

22. The cause of the long response time must be due to the destroyers having to be diverted from other duties before they could join Division Six.

23. A. Claude (*Cassin*) to Sims, report, 18 October 1918, CB File, RG 45.

24. Rodgers to Sims, general report, 17 October 1918, OB File, RG 45. This report includes a copy of all dispatches from Sims and Bayly during this operation.

25. Admiralstab des Marine, "Kriegsoperationen in der Nordsee" and "Zur Geschichte des Admiralstaves im Weltkrieg, 1914–1918," Records of the German Navy; Gladisch and Groos, *Der Krieg in der Nordsee*, vol. 7. Adm. Reinhard Scheer also makes no mention of any plans for a battle cruiser raid; see his memoir, *Germany's High Seas Fleet in the World War* (New York: Peter Smith, 1934).

26. Rodgers to Sims, general report, 26 October 1918, OB File, RG 45.

27. Rodgers to Sims, general report, 10 November 1918, OB File, RG 45.

28. The captains promoted included William H. G. Bullard, A. G. Scales, Henry Wiley, C. F. Hughes, Victor Blue, and Thomas Washington from Division Nine, and Mark Bristol, F. B. Bassett, and A. T. Long from Division Six; Senate Committee on Naval Affairs, *Awarding Medals in the Naval Service: Hearing before a Subcommittee on Naval Affairs*, 66th Cong., 2d sess., 6 June 1919, 40–41.

29. Capt. E. L. Beach was the father of the famous World War II submariner and author of the same name.

30. Rodgers to Sims, general report, 23 November 1918, OB File, RG 45; Rodgers to Sims, general report, 30 November 1918, OB File, RG 45; "United States Battleships in European Waters Including United States Battleships Attached to the British Grand Fleet."

31. Rodgers to Sims, general report, 14 September 1918, OB File, RG 45; "United States Battleships in European Waters Including United States Battleships Attached to the British Grand Fleet."

Chapter 7 / The Twilight of the Great White Fleet

1. Friedman, *U.S. Battleships*, 124–34; Gray, *Conway's, 1906–1921*, 116–17.

2. Miller, *The U.S. Navy: An Illustrated History*, 239–45.

3. Roger Chesneau and Eugene Kolesnik, *Conway's All the World's Fighting Ships, 1860–1905* (New York: Mayflower Books, 1979), 140–44; Friedman, *U.S. Battleships*, 26–49.

4. Gray, *Conway's, 1906–1921*, 112–13; "Historical Sketch of the U.S.S. *Michigan*," historical narrative, 31 August 1923, OS File, RG 45.

5. "Historical Sketch of the U.S.S. *Michigan*"; Senate Committee on Naval Affairs, *Hearings before the Subcommittee of the Committee on Naval Affairs*, 66th Cong., 2d sess., 7 April 1920, 550–51.

6. Benson to Grant, cable, 16 November 1917, OB File, RG 45; Grant to Force One, "System of Training for Force One," memorandum, 22 February 1918, IA File, RG 45.

7. War Diary, Battleship Force One, U.S. Atlantic Fleet, 15 June 1918, OB File, RG 45. Presumably the *Oregon*, *Connecticut*, and *Vermont* remained in reserve.

8. Ibid.

9. Wainwright to Kittelle, memorandum, 14 September 1917, OS File, RG 45.

10. Kittelle to Rear Adm. J. L. Jayne, memorandum, 14 September 1917, OS File, RG 45.

11. Grant to Mayo, report, 18 September 1917, OB File, RG 45.

12. Grant to Mayo, report, 30 January 1918, OB File, RG 45; Commander, *Michigan*, to Commander, Division Five, report, 15 January 1918, OS File, RG 45.

13. Fleet Gunnery Officer to Benson, memorandum, 3 June 1918, OS File, RG 45; McNeely (*Ohio*) to Grant, report, 1 June 1918, OS File, RG 45; Marvell (*Louisiana*) to Grant, report, 2 June 1918, OS File, RG 45; War Diary, Battleship Force One, U.S. Atlantic Fleet, entry for 1 June 1918, OB File, RG 45.

14. There was no U-boat attack that day. The only German submarine operating in U.S. waters then was U-151. It is possible that she had been in the vicinity of the battleships, but improbable that she encountered them. On 2 July, the U-boat commander released prisoners taken from several coastal ships the submarine had sunk earlier. They later testified that U-151 did not make any attacks on 1 June. Marvell (*Louisiana*) to Grant, report, 2 June 1918, OS File, RG 45; McNeely (*Ohio*) to Grant, report, 1 June 1918, OS File, RG 45; "Historical Sketch of the U.S.S. *Louisiana* during the World War," historical narrative, 18 October 1923, OS File, RG 45.

15. Grant, in War Diary, Battleship Force One, U.S. Atlantic Fleet, entry for 7 July 1918, OB File, RG 45.

16. Grant, in War Diary, Battleship Force One, U.S. Atlantic Fleet, entry for 14 July 1918, OB File, RG 45.

17. Grant, in War Diary, Battleship Force One, U.S. Atlantic Fleet, entry for 10 July 1918, OB File, RG 45.

18. Senate Committee on Naval Affairs, *Hearings before the Subcommittee of the Committee on Naval Affairs*, 66th Cong., 2d sess., 7 April 1920, 549, 557.

19. "Historical Sketch of U.S.S. *Minnesota*," historical narrative, n.d., OS File, RG 45; War Diary, Battleship Force One, U.S. Atlantic Fleet, entry for 29 September 1918, OS File, RG 45; Chase (*Minnesota*) to Grant, "Report of Damage Sustained by Striking a Mine," report, 3 October 1918, OS File, RG 45.

20. Instructions regarding operational control are in Grant to Brotherton (*South Carolina*), Movement Orders, OS File, RG 45; Albert Gleaves, *A History of the Transport Service: Adventures and Experiences of United States Transports and Cruisers in the World War* (New York: George Doran Co., 1921).

21. "State of *King Edward VII* Class Battleships in Home Waters," Admiralty memorandum, 15 October 1918, ADM 137/1622, Admiralty Records.

22. Gilmes (*South Carolina*) to Grant, report, 25 September 1918, OS File, RG 45.

23. The Naval Overseas Transportation Service was the U.S. Navy's fleet of merchant vessels that helped supply the logistical needs of the American Expeditionary Force and Navy, including the transport of the mines for the North Sea mine barrage; see Lewis Clephane, *History of the Naval Overseas Transportation Service in World War I* (Washington, D.C.: U.S. Naval History Division, 1969).

24. Gleaves to Burrage (*Nebraska*), Movement Orders, 12 September 1918, OS File, RG 45; "Historical Sketch of the U.S.S. *Nebraska*," n.d., OS File, RG 45.

25. Convoy schedule, "Miscellaneous Convoy and Merchant Marine Information," number 3, series ZO: World War I, Early Records Collection, Operational Archives Branch, Naval Historical Center, Washington Navy Yard, Washington, D.C.; Kittelle (*Georgia*) to Grant, report, 10 October 1918, OS File, RG 45; Executive Officer (*Georgia*) to Kittelle, report, 9 October 1918, OS File, RG 45.

26. Clephane, *Naval Overseas Transportation Service*, 151; Marvell (*Louisiana*) to Grant, report, 20 October 1918; "Historical Sketch of the U.S.S. *Louisiana* during the World War."

27. Clephane, *Naval Overseas Transportation Service*, 151; Sailing Orders to *Michigan*, 28 September 1918, OS File, RG 45; Laws (*Michigan*) to Naval Oper-

ations, cable, 12 October 1918, OS File, RG 45. The cause of the problem is not clear.

28. "Historical Sketch of the U.S.S. *Nebraska.*" The *Edinburgh Castle* was a merchantman that was converted to a warship simply by arming her with 6-inch guns as a cruiser; the *Montana* was armed with four 10-inch guns.

29. "Miscellaneous Convoy and Merchant Marine Information."

30. "Historical Sketch of the U.S.S. *Louisiana* during the World War."

31. Kittelle (*Georgia*) to Grant, report, 22 November 1918, OS File, RG 45; "Miscellaneous Convoy and Merchant Marine Information"; U.S. Navy Department, *Annual Report of the Secretary of the Navy for the Fiscal Year 1918* (Washington, D.C.: GPO, 1918).

32. "Miscellaneous Convoy and Merchant Marine Information."

33. Freeman to Daniels, "War Use for Battleships," memorandum, 28 January 1918, OB File, RG 45.

34. Ibid. Freeman submitted this memorandum through the proper channels and with the approval of his superiors.

35. Benson to Freeman, memorandum, 1 March 1918, OB File, RG 45.

36. Grant to Daniels, "Employment of Battleships for Transporting Troops from Abroad," memorandum, 14 November 1918, OB File, RG 45.

37. Mayo to Benson, cable, 22 November 1918, OB File, RG 45.

38. Benson to Mayo, cable, 24 November 1918, OB File, RG 45.

39. Grant to division commanders, "Transportation of Troops on Battleships of Battleship Force One," orders, 3 December 1918, OB File, RG 45.

40. Commander of U.S. Naval Forces in France (Wilson) to Benson, "Battleships Engaged in Transporting Troops," report, 9 January 1919, Papers of Admiral Benson.

41. Naval Operations to Benson in Paris, cable (excerpts from unnamed Army officer's report, forwarded by U.S. Army director of embarkation), Papers of Admiral Benson.

42. Dillon to Wurtsbaugh (*Nebraska*), letter, 27 January 1919, OS File, RG 45.

43. "U.S.S. *Minnesota*, Transportation of Troops, Interior Regulations and General Information," pamphlet, 10 April 1919, OS File, RG 45.

44. Navy Department, "Memorandum Relative to Number of Troops Carried by Troop-Transport Battleships," 13 March 1919, OB File, RG 45.

45. Clark (*Vermont*) to Mayo, report, n.d., OB File, RG 45.

46. Mayo to Grant and Gleaves, "Operation of Battleships as Troop Transports," memorandum, 30 January 1919, OB File, RG 45.

47. Benson to Grant, cable, 8 February 1919, OB File, RG 45.

48. Grant to Benson, "Transportation of Troops from France to the United States on Board Ships of Battleship Force One," memorandum, 17 March 1919, OB File, RG 45. Grant sent a copy of this memorandum to Gleaves.

49. During their trips from Brest in June 1919 the *Nebraska, Louisiana,* and *Minnesota* transported less than 1,300 troops each; see the historical sketches of those ships.

50. Benson to Grant and Gleaves, memorandum, 16 June 1919, OB File, RG 45.

51. Gleaves, *A History of the Transport Service,* 31.

52. Gray, *Conway's, 1906–1921,* 108–9.

53. "Historical Sketch of the U.S.S. *Minnesota.*"

54. Gray, *Conway's, 1906–1921,* 108–9.

Conclusion

1. Halpern, *A Naval History,* 47–48.

2. The U.S. Navy began with 67,000 officers and men and expanded to nearly 500,000 in World War I—an expansion of 7.5 times. In World War II, the Navy began with nearly 760,000 officers and men and expanded to over 3,250,000—a four-fold expansion. See Samuel Elliot Morison, *The Two Ocean War: A Short History of the United States Navy in the Second World War* (New York: Ballantine Books, 1963), 496.

BIBLIOGRAPHY

✳

Primary Sources
Government Archives

Great Britain. Public Record Office. Cabinet Papers. Minutes, 1916–1922.

———. Cabinet Papers. Committee of Imperial Defense. Series G, 1915–1920.

———. War Cabinet. GT Papers, 1917–1919.

———. Admiralty Records. ADM 137/1436–2710, ADM 116/1342–2068.

United States. National Archives. Records of the Department of the Navy. Naval Records Collection of the Office of Naval Records and Library. Record Group (RG) 74. Records of the Bureau of Ordnance, 1900–1947.

———. RG 45. Subject File 1911–1927. Files: CB, OS, OB, IA, IC, TT, TD, TP.

———. RG 80. General Board Subject File, 1900–1947.

United States. National Archives Branch Depository, College Park, Md. Records of the German Navy, 1850–1945. RG 242. Microfilm publication T-1022.

United States. Naval Historical Center. Operational Archives Branch. Early Records Collection.

United States. Naval War College. Cruiser and Transport Force. Orders for Ships in Convoy, 1918.

———. Operational Archives Branch. Lectures, 1916–1926.

———. Operational Archives Branch. Office of Naval Intelligence. Monthly Information Bulletins, 1918–1919.

Private Papers

Beatty, Admiral of the Fleet, the Earl. Papers. National Maritime Museum, Greenwich, U.K.

Benson, William S. Papers. Manuscript Division, Library of Congress, Washington, D.C.

Daniels, Josephus. Papers. Manuscript Division, Library of Congress, Washington, D.C.

Link, Arthur S. *The Papers of Woodrow Wilson.* Princeton University Press, 1984.

McCrea, Joubert. Diary. U.S. Army Military History Institute, Carlisle Barracks, Pa.

Sims, William. Papers. Manuscript Division, Library of Congress, Washington, D.C.

Wester Wemyss, Lord. Papers. Special Collections, University of California, Irvine (microfilm).

Wilson, Woodrow. Papers. Manuscript Division, Library of Congress, Washington, D.C.

Memoirs and Published Primary Sources

Bayly, Sir Lewis. *Pull Together! The Memoirs of Admiral Sir Lewis Bayly.* London: George Harrap and Co., 1939.

Cronon, Paul. *The Cabinet Diaries of Josephus Daniels.* Lincoln: University of Nebraska Press, 1963.

Daniels, Josephus. *The Wilson Era: Years of War and After, 1917–1923.* Chapel Hill: University of North Carolina Press, 1946.

Fremantle, Sidney. *My Naval Career, 1880–1928.* London: Hutchinson and Co., 1947.

Gleaves, Albert. *The Admiral: The Memoirs of Albert Gleaves, USN.* Pasadena: Hope Publishing House, 1985.

Hurley, Edward. *The Bridge to France.* Philadelphia: J. B. Lippincott Co., 1927.

Jellicoe, Viscount. *The Crisis of the Naval War.* New York: George Doran Co., 1920.

———. *The Grand Fleet, 1914–1916: Its Creation, Development and Work.* New York: George Doran Co., 1919.

Lloyd George, David. *The War Memoirs of David Lloyd George.* 6 vols. Boston: Little, Brown and Co., 1920.

Rodman, Hugh. *Yarns of a Kentucky Admiral.* Indianapolis: Bobbs-Merrill Co., 1928.

Scheer, Reinhard. *Germany's High Seas Fleet in the World War.* New York: Peter Smith, 1934.

Simpson, Michael, ed. *Documents Relating to Anglo-American Naval Relations, 1917–1919.* Brookfield: Naval Records Society, 1991.

Sims, William. *The Victory at Sea.* New York: Doubleday, Page and Co., 1920.

U.S. Navy Department. *Annual Report of the Secretary of the Navy for the Fiscal Year 1918.* Washington, D.C.: GPO, 1918.

———. Office of Naval Intelligence Historical Section. *The American Naval Planning Section in London.* Washington, D.C.: GPO, 1923.

Wiley, Henry A. *An Admiral from Texas.* New York: Doubleday, Doran and Co., 1934.

Secondary Sources
Books and Monographs

Auken, Wilbur. *Notes on a Half Century of United States Naval Ordnance, 1880–1930.* Washington, D.C.: George Banta Publishing Co., 1939.

Beach, Edward. *The United States Navy: 200 Years.* New York: Henry Holt and Co., 1986.

Bell, A. C. *The Blockade of the Central Powers, 1914–1918.* London: Her Majesty's Stationary Office, 1961.

Bennett, Geoffrey. *Naval Battles of the First World War.* London: B. T. Batsford, 1968.

Chesneau, Roger, and Eugene Kolesnik. *Conway's All the World's Fighting Ships, 1860–1905.* New York: Mayflower Books, 1979.

Clephane, Lewis. *History of the Naval Overseas Transportation Service in World War I.* Washington, D.C.: U.S. Naval History Division, 1969.

Coletta, Paolo E. *Sea Power in the Atlantic and Mediterranean in World War I.* New York: University Press of America, 1989.

———. *Admiral Bradley A. Fisk and the American Navy.* Lawrence: Regents Press of Kansas, 1979.

———. *A Survey of U.S. Naval Affairs, 1865–1917.* New York: University Press of America, 1987.

Corbett, Sir Julian, and Henry Newbolt. *History of the Great War: Naval Operations.* 5 vols. New York: Longman, Green and Co., 1920–31.

Friedman, Norman. *U.S. Battleships: An Illustrated Design History.* Annapolis, Md.: Naval Institute Press, 1985.

———. *U.S. Naval Weapon Systems: Every Gun, Mine, and Torpedo Used by the U.S. Navy from 1883 to the Present.* Annapolis, Md.: Naval Institute Press, 1983.

Frothingham, Thomas. *The Naval History of the World War.* New York: Books for Libraries Press, 1924.

Gibbons, Tony. *The Complete Encyclopedia of Battleships: A Technical Directory of Capital Ships from 1860 to the Present Day.* New York: Crescent Books, 1983.

Gladisch, Walther and Otto Groos. *Der Krieg in der Nordsee.* 7 vols. Berlin: E. S. Mittler, 1930.

Gleaves, Albert. *A History of the Transport Service: Adventures and Experiences of United States Transports and Cruisers in the World War.* New York: George Doran Co., 1921.

Gray, Randal, ed. *Conway's All the World's Fighting Ships, 1906–1921*. Annapolis, Md.: Naval Institute Press, 1985.

Hagan, Kenneth. *This People's Navy: The Making of American Sea Power.* New York: Free Press, 1991.

————, ed. *In War and Peace: Interpretations of American Naval History, 1775–1984*. 2d ed. Westport, Conn.: Greenwood Press, 1984.

Halpern, Paul. *A Naval History of World War I*. Annapolis, Md.: Naval Institute Press, 1994.

Hampshire, Arthur Cecil. *The Blockaders*. London: William Kimber & Co., 1980.

Harris, Brayton. *The Age of Battleships*. New York: Franklin Watts, Inc., 1965.

Harrod, Frederick. *Manning the New Navy: The Development of a Modern Naval Enlisted Force, 1899–1940*. Westport, Conn.: Greenwood Press, 1978.

Herwig, Holger. *Luxury Fleet: The Imperial German Navy, 1888–1918*. London: Ashfield Press, 1980.

Hodges, Peter. *The Big Gun: Battleship Main Armament, 1860–1945*. Annapolis, Md.: Naval Institute Press, 1981.

Hoehling, A A *The Great War at Sea: A History of Naval Action, 1914–1918*. New York: Galahad Books, 1965.

Hough, Richard. *The Great War at Sea, 1914–1918*. Oxford University Press, 1983.

————. *Dreadnought: A History of the Modern Battleship*. New York: Bonanza Books, 1979.

Howarth, Stephen. *To Shining Sea: A History of the United States Navy, 1775–1991*. New York: Random House, 1991.

Hurd, Sir Archibald. *History of the Great War: The Merchant Navy*. 3 vols. London: John Murray, 1929.

Jane, Fred T. *Jane's Fighting Ships, 1914*. 1914. Reprint. New York: Arco Publishing Company, 1969.

Keegan, John. *The Price of Admiralty: The Evolution of Naval Warfare*. New York: Penguin Books, 1988.

Kennedy, Paul. *The Rise and Fall of British Naval Mastery*. London: Ashfield Press, 1976.

Klachko, Mary and David Trask. *Admiral William Shepherd Benson: First Chief of Naval Operations*. Annapolis, Md.: Naval Institute Press, 1987.

Legg, Stuart, ed. *Jutland: An Eye Witness Account of a Great Battle*. London: Rupert Hart-Davis, 1966.

Liddle, Peter. *The Sailor's War, 1914–1918*. Dorset: Blandford Press, 1985.

Livezey, William. *Mahan on Sea Power.* Norman: University of Oklahoma Press, 1986.

Love, Robert, Jr. *History of the U.S. Navy, 1775–1941.* Harrisburg: Stockpole Books, 1992.

Mahan, Alfred T. *The Influence of Sea Power on History: 1660–1783.* 12th ed. Boston: Little, Brown and Co., 1918.

Marder, Arthur J. *From the Dreadnought to Scapa Flow: The Royal Navy in the Fisher Era, 1904–1919.* 5 vols. London: Oxford University Press, 1970.

Maurice, Sir Frederick. *Lessons of Allied Cooperation: Naval, Military and Air.* London: Oxford University Press, 1942.

McFarland, Earl. *Textbook of Ordnance and Gunnery.* New York: John Wiley and Sons, 1929.

Miller, Edward. *War Plan Orange: The U.S. Strategy to Defeat Japan, 1897–1945.* Annapolis, Md.: Naval Institute Press, 1991.

Miller, Nathan. *The U.S. Navy: An Illustrated History.* New York: Bonanza Books, 1977.

Morison, Elting. *Admiral Sims and the Modern American Navy.* Boston: Houghton Mifflin Co., 1942.

Morison, Samuel Elliot. *The Two Ocean War: A Short History of the United States Navy in the Second World War.* New York: Ballantine Books, 1963.

Murdock, Lawrence. *They Also Served.* New York: Carlton Press, 1967.

O'Connell, Robert L. *Sacred Vessels: The Cult of the Battleship and the Rise of the U.S. Navy.* New York: Oxford University Press, 1991.

Padfield, Peter. *The Battleship Era.* New York: David McKay Co., 1972.

———. *Guns at Sea.* New York: St. Martin's Press, 1974.

Paret, Peter, ed. *Makers of Modern Strategy: From Machiavelli to the Nuclear Age.* Princeton University Press, 1986.

Potter, E. B. *The Naval Academy Illustrated History of the United States Navy.* New York: Thomas Crowell Co., 1971.

Power, Hugh. *Battleship Texas.* College Station: Texas A&M Press, 1993.

Preston, Antony. *Battleships of World War I: An Illustrated Encyclopedia of the Battleships of All Nations, 1914–1918.* Harrisburg: Stockpole Books, 1972.

Ranft, Bryan. *The Beatty Papers: The Private and Official Correspondence of Admiral of the Fleet Earl Beatty.* Brookfield, Vt.: Scholarly Press, 1989.

Reilly, John C., and Robert L. Scheina. *American Battleships, 1886–1923: Predreadnought Design and Construction.* Annapolis, Md.: Naval Institute Press, 1980.

Reynolds, Clark. *Famous American Admirals.* New York: Van Nostrand-Reinhold Co., 1978.

Roskill, Steven. *Admiral of the Fleet Earl Beatty: The Last Naval Hero.* New York: Atheneum, 1981.

Silverstone, Paul. *U.S. Warships of World War I.* Garden City, N.J.: Doubleday and Co., 1970.

Siney, Marion. *The Allied Blockade of Germany, 1914–1916.* Ann Arbor: University of Michigan Press, 1957.

Sprout, Harold, and Margaret Sprout. *The Rise of American Naval Power, 1776–1918.* Annapolis, Md.: Naval Institute Press, 1990.

Stokesbury, James. *A Short History of World War I.* New York: William Morrow and Co., 1981.

Sumida, Jon. *In Defense of Naval Supremacy: Finance, Technology and British Naval Policy, 1889–1914.* Boston: Unwin Hyman, 1989.

Trask, David. *Captains and Cabinets: Anglo-American Naval Relations, 1917–1918.* Columbia: University of Missouri Press, 1972.

U.S. Naval Institute. *Naval Ordnance: A Textbook Prepared for the Use of the Midshipmen of the United States Naval Academy.* Annapolis, Md.: Naval Institute Press, 1921.

Wegener, Wolfgang. *The Naval Strategy of the World War.* Translated by Holger Herwig. Annapolis, Md.: Naval Institute Press, 1989.

Wheeler, Gerald. *Admiral William Veazie Pratt, U.S. Navy.* Washington, D.C.: Department of the Navy, 1974.

Articles

Allard, Dean C. "Anglo-American Naval Differences during World War I." *Military Affairs* 44 (April 1980): 75–80.

Baer, George. "U.S. Naval Strategy, 1890–1945." *Naval War College Review* 44 (Winter 1991): 6–32.

Blandy, W. H. P. "Possible Improvements in Our Gunnery Training." U.S. Naval Institute *Proceedings* 51 (December 1925): 1696–1702.

Chase, J. V. "Accuracy of Fire at Long Ranges." U.S. Naval Institute *Proceedings* 46 (August 1920): 1175–95.

Gayer, A. "Summary of German Submarine Operations in the Various Theaters of War from 1914–1918." U.S. Naval Institute *Proceedings* 52 (April 1926): 621–59.

Leyman, Charles. "Which It Will Forget at Its Peril." *Sea Power* 15 (September 1972): 33.

McKillip, Robert. "Undermining Technology by Strategy: Resolving the Trade Protection Dilemma of 1917." *Naval War College Review* 44 (Summer 1991): 18–37.

Perkins, F. M. "Is the Fleet Strategically Concentrated?" U.S. Naval Institute *Proceedings* 48 (November 1922): 1883–1906.

Rodman, Hugh. "The Christmas Ship." U.S. Naval Institute *Proceedings* 57 (July 1931): 888.

Simpson, Michael. "Admiral William S. Sims, U.S. Navy, and Admiral Sir Lewis Bayly, Royal Navy: An Unlikely Friendship and Anglo-American Cooperation, 1917–1919." *Naval War College Review* (Spring 1988): 66–80.

Sumida, Jon. "British Capital Ship Design and Fire Control in the *Dreadnought* Era: Sir John Fisher, Arthur Hungerford Pollen, and the Battle Cruiser." *Journal of Modern History* 51 (June 1979): 205–30.

———. "British Naval Administration and Policy in the Age of Fisher." *Journal of Military History* 54 (January 1990): 1–26.

Trask, David. "Woodrow Wilson and the Reconciliation of Force and Diplomacy: 1917–1918." *Naval War College Review* 32 (January 1975): 23–31.

Van Huben, Lewis. "World War I: The Battleships That Didn't Fight." U.S. Naval Institute *Proceedings* 101 (June 1975): 8888–89.

Bibliographical Aids

Allard, Dean, Martha Crawley, and Mary Edmison. *U.S. Naval History Sources in the United States.* Washington, D.C.: Department of the Navy, 1979.

Buckingham, Peter. *Woodrow Wilson: A Bibliography of His Times and Presidency.* Wilmington, Del.: Scholarly Resources, 1990.

Coletta, Paolo. *A Selected and Annotated Bibliography of American Naval History.* New York: University Press of America, 1988.

Kinnell, Susan, ed. *Military History of the United States: An Annotated Bibliography.* Santa Barbara, Calif.: ABC-Clio Press, 1986.

INDEX

✳

Aboukir, HMS (cruiser), 114
Admiralty, 2, 4, 5, 10, 13, 15, 16, 17, 18,
  19, 29, 31, 34, 35, 38, 39, 44, 46, 47, 48,
  49, 50, 51, 52, 58, 69, 79, 81, 86, 89, 93,
  98, 99, 101, 102, 105
  and director firing, 78
  failure to adopt the Pollen fire con-
    trol system, 80
  naval policy, 6–8, 11–12, 22–25, 127
  plans division, 54, 90
  plans to counter German raiders, 91,
    92, 96, 97, 104
  requests U.S. battleships, 9, 12, 14
Agincourt, HMS (battleship), 87
aircraft, 36, 64, 65, 86
Allen, USS (destroyer), 104, 105
Allied Naval Council, 19, 52, 53, 70, 71
American fire control, 79–81
American planning section, 91, 96, 98
American squadron, 22, 25, 27, 28, 30, 31,
  32, 33, 41, 42, 43, 46, 47, 50, 52, 53, 54,
  59, 61, 62, 68, 73, 75, 84, 88, 128. *See
  also* Sixth Battle Squadron; Division Nine
  gunnery deficiencies, 129
  gunnery practice, 67, 86, 87
  maneuvers, 34
  tactical cooperation with the Grand
    Fleet, 76
Andes, HMS (armed merchant cruiser), 120

Argo Clock, 79, 80, 81
Argus, HMS (aircraft carrier), 65
Arizona, USS (battleship), 92, 106
Arkansas, USS (battleship), 40, 41, 42, 61,
  62, 67, 68, 69, 81, 106
Atlantic Fleet, 10, 17, 18, 25, 26, 43, 55,
  56, 83, 86, 92, 100, 106, 110, 113, 117,
  121, 126, 128
  training practices, 84, 85, 111
Aylmer, Capt. H. E. F., 41

Balch, USS (destroyer), 105
Balfour, Arthur James, 5
balloons, 64, 65, 104, 105, 119
Bayly, Adm. Sir Lewis, 101–4
Beach, Capt. E. L., 106
Beale, USS (destroyer), 104
Beatty, Adm. Sir David, 27, 31, 33, 34, 35,
  38, 39, 41, 42, 43, 45, 49, 50, 51, 54, 58,
  60, 61, 63, 65, 66, 67, 70, 71, 72, 73, 74,
  77
  concern over U.S. battleship deficien-
    cies, 32, 44
  and Grand Fleet policy, 23, 24, 28–30
  relations with Rodman, 75
Belknap, Capt. Reginald, 56
Benson, Adm. William Shepard, 2, 3, 8, 11,
  12, 13, 14, 15, 17, 18, 20, 26, 38, 39, 41,
  47, 51, 90, 91, 93, 121, 122, 125

Benson, Adm. William Shepard (*cont.*)
appointment as Chief of Naval Operations, 19
concern over risking U.S. battleships to escort Scandinavian convoys, 46
decides to send battleships to Britain, 16
mission to England, 16
places priority on protecting troop convoys, 89
plans to counter German raiders, 96
reluctance to send U.S. battleships to Europe, 10
Berehaven (Ireland), 18, 95, 96, 97, 98, 100, 102, 103, 104, 105, 106, 107, 111
Blue, Capt. Victor, 38, 39, 40
Brainard, Capt. R. M., 88
Bremse, SMS (light cruiser), 34
Bristol, Capt. Mark, 100
British blockade, 4, 11–12, 22–23
British fire control, 79–81
Browning, Vice Adm. Sir Montague E., 2
Brummer, SMS (light cruiser), 34
Bullard, Capt. W. H. G., 61, 62
Bureau of Ordnance, 80, 81

Canandaigua, USS (liner converted to minelayer), 56
Canonicus, USS (liner converted to mine-layer), 56
Cardiff, HMS (light cruiser), 72
Cassin, USS (destroyer), 105
Christy, Capt. H. H., 106
Churchill, Winston (U.S. journalist), 6, 7, 15, 108
close-blockade, 2, 4, 5, 7, 11, 127
Cole, Capt. W. C., 106
Connecticut, USS (pre-dreadnought), 110
Conqueror, HMS (battleship), 87
convoys, 5, 6, 9, 15, 18, 23, 24, 25, 34, 35, 44, 46, 47, 48, 49, 50, 51, 57, 69, 89, 90, 91, 92, 93, 96, 97, 98, 99, 100, 102, 104, 105, 107, 108, 117, 119, 120, 128, 129
Conyngham, USS (destroyer), 104
Cressy, HMS (cruiser), 114

Daniels, Secretary of the Navy Josephus, 2, 4, 5, 7, 11, 13, 16, 17, 18, 19, 25, 33, 40, 42, 120, 121
and battleship operations, 26
chooses first Chief of Naval Operations, 20
criticism of the Admiralty, 10
on naval policy, 6, 8
refuses to grant Rodman a promotion, 52
Davis, USS (destroyer), 106
De Chair, Rear Adm. Dudley, 5
de Grasse, Rear Adm. Maurice Ferdinand Albert, 2
Delaware, USS (battleship), 17, 25, 26, 27, 28, 32, 37, 38, 40, 41, 42, 46, 47, 57, 59, 61, 62, 88, 116
Dent, USS (destroyer), 118, 120
Derfflinger, SMS (battle cruiser), 95
Desteiger, Capt. L. R., 106
director firing, 77–78
Division Nine, 17, 18, 25, 26, 27, 29, 39, 101, 106, 111, 128. *See also* American squadron; Sixth Battle Squadron
Division Six, 18, 92, 95, 96, 100, 101, 102, 103, 106, 107
operations, 104, 105
Dover Patrol, 5, 32, 44
Down, Cdr. Richard, 86
Downes, USS (destroyer), 104, 106
Drayton, Capt. John, 106
Dreyer system, 79
Duncan, USS (destroyer), 106

Earle, Rear Adm. Ralph, 80
Edinburgh Castle, HMS (armed merchant cruiser), 120
Emden, SMS (light cruiser), 35
Erin, HMS (battleship), 87
Evan-Thomas, Vice Adm. Hugh, 62, 63

fire control, 29, 42, 54, 72, 78, 79, 80, 81, 84, 86, 87, 103, 106, 114
Fisk, Adm. Bradley R., 78
Florida, USS (battleship), 17, 26, 27, 28,

32, 37, 38, 40, 41, 46, 57, 59, 62, 63, 67, 68, 71, 81, 88, 101, 106
Foch, Marshall Ferdinand, 71
Force One, 110, 111, 113, 114, 117, 124, 125
  used as transports, 122
Force Two, 110, 111
Ford Rangekeeper, 80, 81
Freeman, Cdr. C. S., 120, 121
Fremantle, Rear Adm. Sidney, 43, 44, 54
Fuller, Capt. C. T., 98

Geddes, Sir Eric, 10, 13, 24, 97
General Board, 14, 15, 20
George Washington, USS (transport), 106, 107
Georgia, USS (pre-dreadnought), 112, 118, 120, 122, 124
German fleet, 7, 8, 11, 23, 48, 49, 50, 68, 69, 70, 71, 73, 74, 76, 106, 127, 128. *See also* High Seas Fleet
German gunnery, 78
Gleaves, Rear Adm. Albert, 117, 124, 125
Gompers, Samuel, 61
Grand Fleet, 4, 9, 11, 12, 13, 14, 16, 17, 18, 26, 27, 28, 30, 33, 35, 38, 39, 40, 42, 44, 46, 47, 49, 50, 51, 52, 53, 54, 55, 56, 58, 60, 61, 62, 64, 65, 68, 69, 70, 71, 72, 77, 78, 82, 83, 85, 86, 87, 88, 101, 106, 111, 128, 129
  battle instructions, 29
  cooperation of U.S. battleships with, 73–76
  gunnery, 80
  high morale, 59
  importance to naval strategy, 7, 10, 22–25, 76, 127
  plans to counter German raiders, 91
  training practices, 84
Grant, Vice Adm. A. W., 112, 113, 114, 115, 116, 121, 124, 125

Heligoland, 18, 23, 47, 48, 127
Hewitt, Cdr. Henry K., 86, 88
High Seas Fleet, 7, 9, 18, 19, 22, 33, 49, 50, 56, 59, 65, 69, 72, 73, 108, 126, 127. *See also* German Fleet
  last sortie, 48
  mutiny, 70
  surrender of, 71
Hipper, Adm. Franz, 69, 70, 71
Hogue, HMS (cruiser), 114
Housatonic, USS (liner converted to mine-layer), 56
House, Col. Edward M., 16, 35, 62
Hughes, Capt. Charles F., 25

Illinois, USS (pre-dreadnought), 109, 126
Indiana, USS (pre-dreadnought), 109, 121
influenza, 68, 69, 105, 118
Iron Duke, HMS (battle cruiser), 31, 42

Jellicoe, Adm. Sir John, 4, 8, 9, 11, 13, 14, 24, 35, 53
joint naval planning section, 19
Jutland, 22, 23, 30, 56, 66, 78, 84

Kansas, USS (pre-dreadnought), 117, 120, 122, 125
Kearsarge, USS (pre-dreadnought), 109, 110, 121, 126
Kentucky, USS (pre-dreadnought), 25, 109
Kilkis (former USS *Idaho*), 110
Kimberly, USS (destroyer), 105
Kimmel, Cdr. Husband E., 83
King Alfred, HMS (pre-dreadnought), 90
King George V, 32, 60
Kinkaid, Lt. Cdr. Thomas C., 80, 84, 87
Kittelle, Capt. S. E., 112, 113, 119

Lansing, Secretary of State Robert, 8
Lansing-Ishii Agreement, 1, 14
Lemnos (former USS *Mississippi*), 110
Leviathan, USS (transport), 69, 90
Long, Capt. A. T., 100, 111
Louisiana, USS (pre-dreadnought), 115, 119, 120, 122, 129
  gunnery accident, 114
  tests Pollen system, 81
Ludendorff, Gen. Erich, 89

Mahan, Adm. Alfred Thayer, 1, 3, 4, 6, 7,
10, 14, 15, 17, 20, 108, 128, 129
Maine, USS (pre-dreadnought), 109
Manley, USS (destroyer), 26, 27
Marlborough, HMS (battle cruiser), 42
Mary Rose, HMS (destroyer), 35
Massachusetts, USS (pre-dreadnought), 109
Maurice, Sir Frederick, 22
Mayo, Adm. Henry T., 11, 12, 14, 15, 106,
113, 122
    inspects the Sixth Battle Squadron, 83
    mission to England, 10, 13
    objects to using pre-dreadnoughts as
    transports, 121
    visits Berehaven, 102
McCall, USS (destroyer), 105, 106
McCrea, Vice Adm. John, 25, 26, 68, 75,
100
McCrea, Joubert, 71, 73
McVay, Capt. C. V., 106
Michigan, USS (battleship), 110, 113, 119
mine barrage, 11, 18, 19, 32, 90
Mine Squadron One, 56
Minnesota, USS (pre-dreadnought), 116,
123, 126
Mississippi, USS (pre-dreadnought), 110
Missouri, USS (pre-dreadnought), 110
Moewe, SMS (commerce raider), 89
Moltke, SMS (battle cruiser), 49
Montana, USS (armored cruiser), 118, 120,
122
Morison, Elting, 77

naval intelligence, 29, 35, 47, 48, 50, 93
naval offensive, 2, 11, 19, 44
Navy Department, 9, 11, 12, 14, 15, 16, 18,
19, 20, 25, 26, 33, 38, 39, 40, 42, 47, 51,
53, 56, 57, 68, 77, 78, 81, 82, 83, 87, 90,
91, 93, 95, 98, 99, 101, 106, 108, 110,
113, 119, 122, 126, 128
    agrees to send battleships to European
    waters, 17
    begins cooperation with the British, 1–3
    criticism of Admiralty policy, 6–7, 10
    and gunnery methods, 85, 86

mobilization and training, 111, 116
naval policy at the outbreak of war, 3–7
plans to counter German raiders, 92,
96, 97, 100, 102, 103, 104
unwillingness to send battleships to European waters, 13
uses pre-dreadnoughts as escorts, 117
uses pre-dreadnoughts as transports, 121
Nebraska, USS (pre-dreadnought), 118,
120, 123, 126
Nevada, USS (battleship), 28, 40, 92, 95,
100, 101, 104, 105, 106, 108
New Hampshire, USS (pre-dreadnought),
114, 115, 117, 122, 129
New Mexico, USS (battleship), 92, 108,
109, 111
New York, USS (battleship), 17, 25, 26, 27,
28, 31, 32, 33, 36, 37, 38, 39, 40, 43, 45,
46, 58, 59, 61, 63, 64, 67, 68, 73, 81, 82,
88, 91, 96, 101, 106, 111, 117, 118
    collides with a German submarine, 66
    during surrender of the German fleet,
    72
    influenza cases among crew, 69
    visit by King George V, 60, 72
North Dakota, USS (armored cruiser), 40,
113
Northcliffe, Lord Alfred, 8
Norway, 11, 17, 33, 34, 36, 39, 90

Oak, HMS (destroyer), 60, 72
Ohio, USS (pre-dreadnought), 114, 115, 121
Oklahoma, USS (battleship), 40, 92, 95,
100, 101, 104, 105, 106
Olmstead, Capt. P. N., 126
Oregon, USS (pre-dreadnought), 109, 126
Orion, HMS (battleship), 87
Otranto, HMS (merchant cruiser), 119

Page, Walter, 52
Partridge, HMS (destroyer), 35
Paulding, USS (destroyer), 105
Pellew, USS (destroyer), 35
Pennsylvania, USS (battleship), 88, 92, 106,
108, 109

Plans Division, 54, 90, 91, 95, 98
  plans for countering German raiders, 93, 96
Pollen, Arthur, 79, 80, 81
Pratt, Capt. William Veazie, 12, 13, 14, 15, 20, 98

Queen Elizabeth, HMS (battleship), 27, 28, 31, 60, 61, 72

raiders, 3, 4, 6, 15, 23, 34, 35, 57, 66, 89, 90, 91, 104, 105, 107, 119
rangefinders, 78, 79, 81
Rhode Island, USS (pre-dreadnought), 122
Rochester, USS (armed merchant cruiser), 118, 120
Rodgers, Rear Adm. Thomas S., 95, 96, 101, 104, 105
  commands Division Six, 100
  relations with Bayly, 102, 103
Rodman, Rear Adm. Hugh, 17, 26, 27, 28, 34, 36, 38, 39, 40, 41, 42, 45, 46, 52, 54, 55, 57, 58, 59, 61, 62, 64, 66, 67, 68, 72, 75, 77, 82, 83, 87
  on British policy and methods, 33, 53
  chosen to command the American squadron with the Grand Fleet, 25
  concern over using battleships to escort Norwegian convoys, 50
  criticizes U.S. gunnery methods, 43
  criticizes U.S. gunnery practices, 85
  Navy Department refuses his advancement to Vice Admiral, 51
  receives Order of the Bath, 60
  relations with Beatty, 74
  testimony before Senate committee, 85
  on U.S. battleship deficiencies, 81
Rosyth (British battle cruiser base), 17, 18, 31, 44, 45, 47, 48, 49, 59, 60, 62, 63, 65, 67, 74, 106
Royal Navy, 4, 6, 8, 10, 12, 14, 25, 31, 60, 101, 129

Samson, USS (destroyer), 104

San Francisco (cruiser converted to minelayer), 56
Scales, Capt. Archibald, 25, 38
Scapa Flow (Grand Fleet base), 17, 18, 19, 26, 27, 29, 31, 33, 36, 37, 39, 43, 44, 45, 46, 58, 60, 62, 63, 65, 66, 67, 71
Scheer, Adm. Reinhard, 48, 49, 50, 69, 70
Schofield, Capt. Frank S., 15
Scott, Sir Percy, 78
Seeadler, SMS (commerce raider), 89
Sims, Vice Adm. William Sowden, 10, 11, 12, 16, 19, 20, 26, 38, 39, 41, 42, 46, 47, 50, 51, 52, 72, 77, 85, 90, 92, 95, 96, 101, 102, 103, 104, 106
  advises battleship escort for troop convoys, 91, 93
  advocacy of convoy system, 5, 6
  on gunnery training, 84
  mission to England, 2
  testimony before Senate committee, 13
  urges concentration in European waters, 4, 5, 7, 8, 9, 14
Sixth Battle Squadron, 27, 28, 38, 39, 40, 41, 46, 48, 51, 53, 58, 59, 61, 63, 72, 74, 83, 101. *See also* American squadron; Division Nine
  contribution to the Grand Fleet, 25, 55, 128
  gunnery practice, 31, 43, 54, 64
  maneuvers, 30, 33, 65
  operations, 36, 42, 45, 47, 49, 56, 62, 66
  position in the British battle line, 29
Snowden, Rear Adm. Thomas, 112
South Carolina, USS (battleship), 110, 117, 118, 120
South Dakota, USS (armored cruiser), 119, 122
St. Louis, USS (armored cruiser), 119, 122
Stavanger, 17, 36, 45
Sterett, USS (destroyer), 106
Stevens, USS (destroyer), 104
Stockton, USS (destroyer), 106
Strauss, Rear Adm. Joseph, 57
Strongbow, HMS (destroyer), 34, 35
submarines, 1–9, 11–12, 18–19, 22, 24, 30,

submarines (*cont.*)
33, 35–38, 43, 44, 47, 48, 57, 58, 62, 63,
64, 66, 67, 69, 71, 89, 91, 93, 102, 103,
114, 115, 119, 127

Talbot, USS (destroyer), 120
Taylor, USS (destroyer), 106
Terry, USS (destroyer), 104, 106
Teutonic, HMS (armed merchant cruiser),
120
Texas, USS (battleship), 38, 39, 40, 45, 46,
47, 57, 60, 65, 67, 68, 73, 78, 81, 82, 113
poor gunnery performance, 43, 85
Transport Force, 117, 124
Trippe, USS (destroyer), 106

U.S. battleships
British request for, 14
comparison with British ships, 81
contribution to the Grand Fleet, 25, 55,
128
fire control, 80
gunnery deficiencies, 82
U-70 (German submarine), 58
U-80 (German submarine), 38

U-82 (German submarine), 38
UB-123 (German submarine), 67
U-boats, 1, 4, 5, 15. *See also* submarines
Ulysses, HMS (destroyer), 63
Undine, HMS (destroyer), 63
Utah, USS (battleship), 40, 92, 95, 100,
101, 102, 104, 105, 106

Vermont, USS (pre-dreadnought), 110, 124
Vickers director, 79
Virginia, USS (pre-dreadnought), 26, 110,
111, 113, 120, 122, 124

Wainwright, John, 112
Washington, Capt. Thomas, 26, 38
Wemyss, Sir Rosslyn Wester, 24, 32, 33, 44,
70, 73
Wiley, Capt. Henry A., 26, 30, 37, 38, 45,
58
Wilson, President Woodrow, 1–2, 5, 6, 7,
10, 11, 15, 19, 52, 69, 106, 107, 108
Wolf, SMS (commerce raider), 89
Wyoming, USS (battleship), 17, 26, 27, 28,
30, 32, 37, 40, 45, 46, 49, 57, 58, 61, 62,
67, 68, 81, 88, 106

About the Author

Jerry W. Jones is Assistant Professor of History and Government at the University of Central Texas. He received his Ph.D. from the University of North Texas in 1995. He resides in Belton, Texas, with his wife, Marie.

*

The **Naval Institute Press** is the book-publishing arm of the U.S. Naval Institute, a private, nonprofit, membership society for sea service professionals and others who share an interest in naval and maritime affairs. Established in 1873 at the U.S. Naval Academy in Annapolis, Maryland, where its offices remain today, the Naval Institute has members worldwide.

Members of the Naval Institute support the education programs of the society and receive the influential monthly magazine *Proceedings* and discounts on fine nautical prints and on ship and aircraft photos. They also have access to the transcripts of the Institute's Oral History Program and get discounted admission to any of the Institute-sponsored seminars offered around the country.

The Naval Institute also publishes *Naval History* magazine. This colorful bimonthly is filled with entertaining and thought-provoking articles, first-person reminiscences, and dramatic art and photography. Members receive a discount on *Naval History* subscriptions.

The Naval Institute's book-publishing program, begun in 1898 with basic guides to naval practices, has broadened its scope in recent years to include books of more general interest. Now the Naval Institute Press publishes about 100 titles each year, ranging from how-to books on boating and navigation to battle histories, biographies, ship and aircraft guides, and novels. Institute members receive discounts of 20 to 50 percent on the Press's nearly 600 books in print.

Full-time students are eligible for special half-price membership rates. Life memberships are also available.

For a free catalog describing Naval Institute Press books currently available, and for further information about subscribing to *Naval History* magazine or about joining the U.S. Naval Institute, please write to:

Membership Department
U.S. Naval Institute
118 Maryland Avenue
Annapolis, MD 21402-5035

Telephone: (800) 233-8764
Fax: (410) 269-7940
Web address: www.usni.org